The Route of the Torbay Express

London Paddington to Paignton & Kingswear (for Dartmouth)

Alexander J. Naughton

Copyright © Alexander J. Naughton 2026

All Rights Reserved

No part of this publication may be reproduced, distributed, or transmitted in any form or by any means, including photocopying, recording, or other electronic or mechanical methods, without the author's prior written permission, except in the case of brief quotations embodied in critical reviews and certain other non-commercial uses permitted by copyright law. For permission requests, please get in touch with the author.

Contents

- Acknowledgements: i
- About the Author ii
- Introduction: 2
- Route Description: 14
  - London Paddington to Reading: 19
  - Reading to Taunton: 24
  - Taunton to Exeter St Davids: 36
  - Exeter St Davids to Paignton: 44
  - Paignton Queens Park to Kingswear (for Dartmouth) 60
- The Destinations 79
  - Torquay 79
  - Paignton 85
  - Brixham 87
  - Dartmouth 92
- Devon's Walking Trails 101
- References: 105
- Image Information: 106

Acknowledgements:

Writing a book is a complex and time consuming task, so I would like to thank my family and friends for their support and encouragement. The majority of the photos in the book are from my own collections, but for the historic archive photos and travel posters I would like to thank the Science Museum Group's Science & Society Picture Library (https://www.scienceandsociety.co.uk/), Network Rail (https://www.networkrail.co.uk/), Colour Rail (https://colourrail.co.uk/), Alamy (https://www.alamy.com), and Great Western Railway (https://www.gwr.com/) for their assistance and use of these images.

Lastly I would thank Sara Taylor (Senior Book Publishing and Marketing Consultant), Helen Cooper (Project Manager), the marketing team and the editorial team at Savvy Book Marketing in Liverpool for their expertise, knowledge and professionalism in helping with the graphic design, social media and website aspects as well as their help in editing and formatting the book so that it can be published, put on retail platforms and printed on demand. They have been a great help.

About the Author

I have over 20 years of experience working professionally in local government in the UK, involved in strategic policy & strategy and devolution with a particular focus on placemaking, transport, climate, environment and nature policy, and have a good understanding of the public sector framework and regularly liaise and collaborate with academia and the private and voluntary sectors.

I have valuable skills, including strategy development, big picture strategic thinking, global trends and horizon scanning, innovation, spatial planning, placemaking, product development, marketing, transport & mobility, etc. I have the ability to think holistically and collaboratively through an ambition-led "vision and validate" approach informed by evidence and data. Key thing is to take a holistic, inclusive, place, and whole economy approach to the future of transport to create better places and healthier lives for everyone. I am keen to foster collaboration, engagement and a community enabling approach.

My personal interests include transport, photography, architecture & design, etc. I am also a transport author with this series of "Through the Window" Rail Guides. I strongly believe that, today, with the hectic pace of modern life, technology at our fingertips, and everyone all too often glued to their smartphones, we risk forgetting the simple pleasures of looking out of the window and enjoying slow travel to experience our surroundings.

These "Through the Window" Rail Guides aim to recapture something of this lost art of travel and encourage people to take time to look out of the window to see the passing places, history, culture, landscapes and natural wonders from the train. I see a train journey as linking a string of pearls and showcasing places you pass as well as the destinations you are travelling to. So I hope you enjoy my endeavours!

Introduction

Introduction:

Today, with the hectic pace of modern life, technology at our fingertips, and everyone all too often glued to their smartphones, we risk forgetting the simple pleasures of looking out of the window and enjoying slow travel to experience our surroundings. It is good to take a moment to step back, reflect and enjoy life. Take a break from your stressful lives, centre yourself and consider your health & wellbeing. Get out there to explore and discover the sights, sounds and experiences across the country.

These "Through the Window" Travel Guides aim to recapture something of this lost art of travel and encourage people to take time to look out of the window to see the passing places, history, culture, landscapes and natural wonders from the train. We see a train journey as linking a string of pearls and showcasing places you pass as well as the destinations you are travelling to. Look around you and admire some of the wonderful railway architecture to be found in the UK. Take a trip to the seaside for a relaxing dip, meet up with friends for a vibrant city break, or simply get back to nature and enjoy some lovely walks in the countryside. So sit back, relax and enjoy your rail journey through Great Britain and its wonderful places and landscapes.

This book focusses on the route from London Paddington to Torquay, Paignton and Kingswear (for Dartmouth) via the Great Western Main Line. This route was made famous by the Torbay Express introduced in 1923 by the Great Western Railway. The publicity by the GWR in the 1930s was legendary, and the Holiday Line and the coastal resorts of Torquay, Paignton and Brixham centred around Tor Bay in South Devon became defined as the English Riviera.

The service was hauled by steam locomotives such as the Castle and King class locomotives until 1958 when diesel locomotives were introduced, such as the Class 41 Warships, Class 42 Warships, Class 52 Westerns, Class 50 Hoovers and Class 47 diesel locomotives. In 1972, British Rail decided to close the route beyond Paignton, and this last section between Paignton and Kingswear is now home to the Dartmouth Steam Railway. The Torbay Express, therefore was truncated to terminate instead at Paignton. In 1981 the Intercity 125 High Speed Trains were introduced onto the service and continued until replaced in 2018 by the Hitachi IEP Class 802 bi-mode trains. The service continues today between London and Paignton under the privatised railways and is now operated by the Great Western Railway.

In late 2027, the newly nationalised Great British Railways (GBR) will take over the operation of most of Britain's passenger train services, stations, and infrastructure, except for devolved train operators, open-access train operators, and local tram and light rail services.

Devolved train operators include Merseyrail, Transport for London, Scottish Rail Holdings, (including ScotRail and Caledonian Sleeper), Transport for Wales, and Translink NI. Open-access operators include Lumo, Hull Trains, Grand Central Rail, and Eurostar.

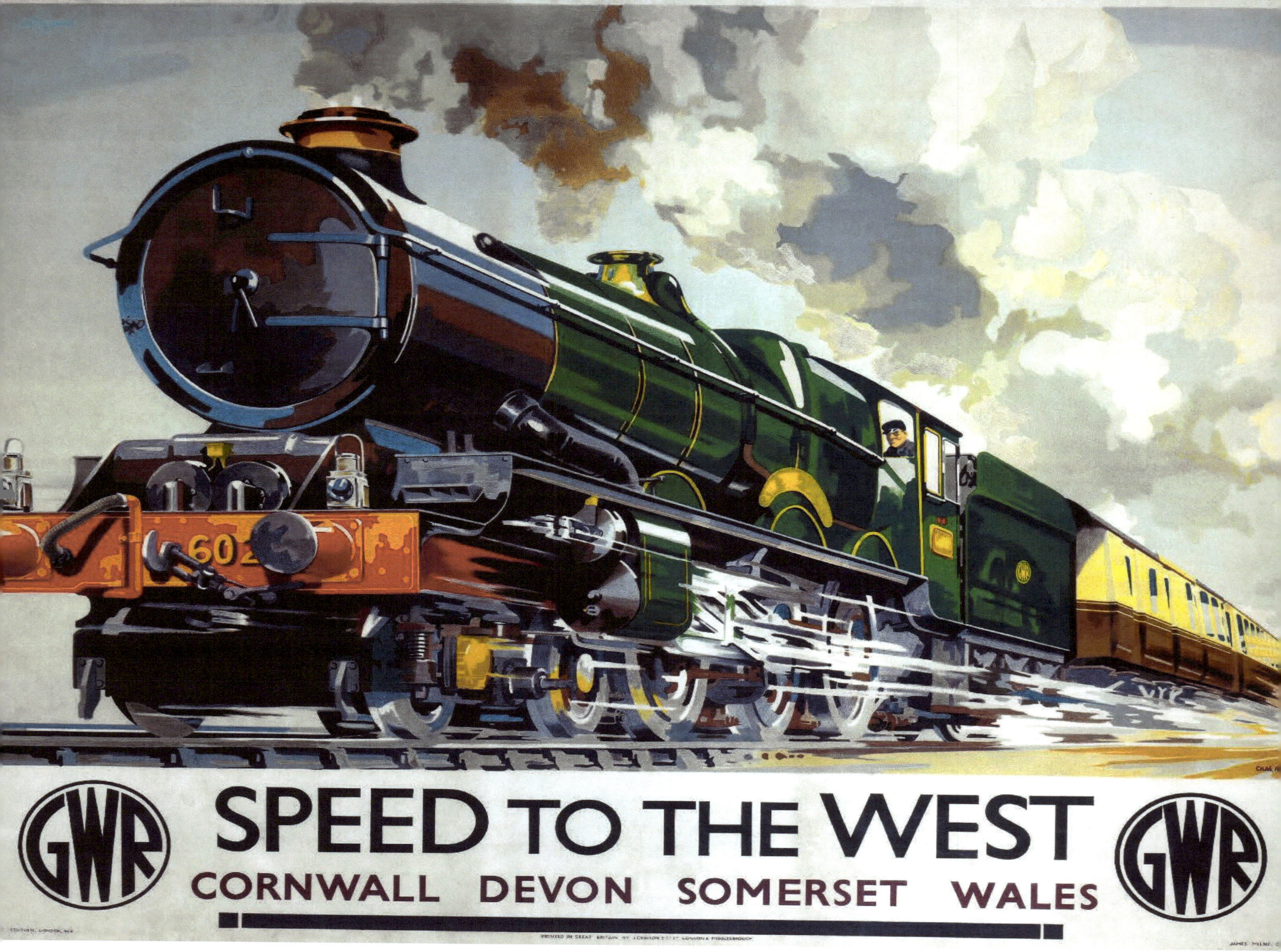

 **SPEED TO THE WEST**
CORNWALL   DEVON   SOMERSET   WALES

The destination, of course, is the English Riviera coastal resorts and Dartmouth. Three bustling seaside towns make up Torbay, also known as the English Riviera. Torquay, Paignton and Brixham each offer something unique. Torquay is a traditional seaside resort famed for its iconic palm trees, busy harbour, international marina, sandy beach and wonderful array of continental-style cafes, restaurants and cocktail bars. Paignton is renowned for its long stretch of beautiful and easily accessible beachfront, promenade, traditional pier, colourful beach huts and green. Life in the busy Devon fishing town of Brixham has always centred around the harbour, where heritage trawlers jostle for space with dayboats heading out to sea for the day's catch, bringing it home daily to Brixham's famous Fish Market. Here, in the heart of England's Seafood Coast, the freshest fish and most delicious seafood is on the menu everywhere. Devon's beautiful English Riviera is set within a sheltered bay with stunning coastal scenery. The rich geological landscape is so unique that it has received international recognition and is a designated UNESCO Global Geopark, one of only 8 in the UK and 140 in the world. It's a deeply indented horseshoe-shaped bay with lots of beaches and coves sheltering wonderful marine life, including seals, porpoises, dolphins and a huge variety of sea birds, including the famous guillemot colony at Berry Head. The English Riviera is set around a large horseshoe-shaped bay and sheltered by the rolling hills of Dartmoor - both of which provide a warm microclimate and safe, shallow waters. Its long sandy beaches, secluded coves and crystal clear waters create a Mediterranean vibe, and mean that water-based activities are the favourite thing to do for both locals and visitors.

Famed for both its maritime and engineering importance, Dartmouth is a town full of culture, history and heritage, from castles to forts, ancient buildings and museums. Dartmouth dates back as far as 1147, and over the centuries has managed to retain many of its original features – though now somewhat modified to fit in with modern life. Just wandering through the streets of Dartmouth, you will see an eclectic mix of architecture amongst the buildings and streets, many dating back to the 16th century, such as the Butterwalk buildings. With castles, forts, and even links to the Mayflower and the founding fathers of America, Dartmouth's maritime heritage is impressive. Even today, Dartmouth is of maritime strategic importance, and is home to the Britannia Royal Naval College that trains the officers of the Royal Navy.

The whole area has strong cultural and literary connections with Dame Agatha Christie, too with her former home at Greenway House being close to Dartmouth. Agatha Christie was born in Torquay and remained on the English Riviera for much of her life. As a result of her love and extensive knowledge of the area, many of her books were either set locally or inspired by the surrounding Devon scenery. Famed as the "Queen of Crime", Agatha Christie's books have sold more than two billion copies, and she remains the most successful female playwright of all time. The experiences, places, and people that she encountered on the English Riviera provided the inspiration for many of the characters and plots she created. Now, every September, the annual International Agatha Christie Festival takes place on the English Riviera, celebrating the life of the Queen of Crime and her legacy.

In the UK our most outstanding natural landscapes which are highly valued for their unrivalled beauty are designated as either National Parks or National Landscapes.

Devon is proud to have two National Parks.

Dartmoor National Park
https://www.dartmoor.gov.uk

Exmoor National Park
https://www.exmoor-nationalpark.gov.uk

Additionally Devon is proud to have a number of National Landscapes including:

Tamar Valley National Landscape
https://www.tamarvalley-nl.org.uk

South Devon National Landscape
https://www.southdevon-nl.org.uk

North Devon Coast National Landscape
https://www.northdevoncoast-nl.org.uk

East Devon National Landscape
https://www.eastdevon-nl.org.uk

Blackdown Hills National Landscape
https://blackdownhillsaonb.org.uk

Also uniquely North Devon is home to the UK's only World Surfing Reserve.

North Devon World Surfing Reserve
https://www.northdevonsurfreserve.org

The North Devon World Surfing Reserve covers a world-class surf zone stretching across approximately 30 km of coastline. Its high density of outstanding surf, at iconic breaks such as Croyde, Saunton, Woolacombe, and Lynmouth, caters to wave-riders of all tastes and styles. The Reserve is the first of its kind in the UK, and only the second in Europe. It is also the first ever cold water World Surfing Reserve, with many of the best waves arriving on the North Devon shoreline in the winter season.

Devon also is home to one of the UK's few UNESCO Global Geoparks:

English Riviera UNESCO Global Geopark
http://www.englishrivierageopark.org.uk

The English Riviera UNESCO Global Geopark has been created over the millennia: it is a place where earth and sea come together, a unification of many worlds and habitats. The 22 miles of coast have been shaped by natural processes to create the environment we know today, providing homes and holidays for people past and present. The diverse landscape encompasses natural caves, beaches, green rolling hills, red sandy rocks, dramatic limestone headlands and sparkling blue seas. The ever-changing light and weather patterns across Torbay work to create an evocative canvas and backdrop to this remarkable place which contains natural caves that were once home to some of Britain's first people. It continues to inspire explorers, scientists, writers and artists, alongside pioneering engineering, fishing and farming communities. A variety of innovative local businesses provide unique opportunities to connect with this magical place. The purpose of a Geopark is to explore, develop and celebrate the links between their geological heritage and all other aspects of the area's natural, cultural and intangible heritage. It also encompasses one of the UK's major tourism areas and is one of the UK's only two "urban" Geoparks.

Lastly Devon is home to one of the UK's few UNESCO Biosphere Reserves.

North Devon UNESCO Biosphere Reserve

https://www.northdevonbiosphere.org.uk

The North Devon UNESCO Biosphere Reserves covers a myriad of diverse landscapes in North Devon from rivers Taw and Torridge to North Devon coast and Lundy Island. At its core is one of the largest sand dune systems in Europe at Braunton Burrows. To the west in Bideford Bay (visible from the beach element of the dunes, Saunton Sands which is a due-west facing surfing beach) is a coral reef with a diversity of coral and marine life seen nowhere else in Britain. The sand dunes have a rich habitat of hundreds of flowering plants while the Taw-Torridge estuary is an important feeding area for long-journey migratory birds. It celebrates the connection between the people, land and the sea.

> **FUN FACT: DID YOU KNOW THAT…..**
>
> Devon famously has an ongoing rivalry with the neighbouring royal duchy and county of Cornwall about how best to do a cream tea which consists of a cup of tea and a scone with clotted cream and jam. The heart of the lengthy and fierce debate rests around what is the correct order to put the layers of clotted cream and jam on the scone! Cornwall says that it is the jam first and then the clotted cream! While Devon says that it is the clotted cream first and then the jam! But do take time to enjoy a classic Cornish cream tea or Devonshire cream tea as either option shouldn't be missed!

FORMER RAILWAY OWNED HOTELS:

The railway companies used to own hotels across their networks to encourage travellers to use the railways for business and leisure and encourage tourism. Some were city centre hotels; others were resort hotels or located at ferry and ocean liner ports. Some survived to become part of British Transport Hotels in 1962. Eventually this was privatised in 1983.

The surviving former railway owned hotels in the Great Western area include:

- Great Western Royal Hotel (GWR London Paddington) now Hilton London Paddington
- Great Western Hotel (GWR Reading) now the Malmaison Reading
- Great Western Hotel (GWR Taunton)
- Fishguard Bay Hotel (GWR Fishguard Harbour)
- Great Western Hotel (GWR Torquay) now Grand Hotel Torquay
- Manor House Hotel (GWR Moretonhampstead) now Bovey Castle Hotel
- Duke of Cornwall Hotel (GWR Plymouth Millbay Docks)
- Great Western Hotel (GWR Newquay)
- Fowey Hotel (GWR Fowey) now Harbour Hotel Fowey
- Falmouth Hotel (GWR Falmouth)
- Tregenna Castle Hotel (GWR St Ives)
- Queens Hotel (GWR Penzance)
- Metropole Hotel (SR Padstow) now Harbour Hotel Padstow

Great Western Royal Hotel, London Paddington
(now Hilton London Paddington)
(c) National Railway Museum / Science Museum

Falmouth Hotel, Falmouth (c) Author's Collection

Tregenna Castle Hotel, St Ives
(c) National Railway Museum / Science Museum Group

Metropole Hotel, Padstow (now Harbour Hotel Padstow) (c) Author's Collection

Manor House Hotel, Moretonhampstead (now Bovey Castle Hotel)
(c) National Railway Museum / Science Museum Group

Fishguard Bay Hotel, Fishguard Harbour
(c) National Railway Museum / Science Museum Group

Great Western Hotel, Torquay (now Grand Hotel Torquay) (c) Author's Collection

Duke of Cornwall Hotel, Plymouth Millbay Docks (c) Author's Collection

Route Description

Route Description:

London Paddington is one of London's grandest and most elegant stations and is an important monument to the work of Isambard Kingdom Brunel. It was built by the Great Western Railway in 1854 and was designed by the legendary engineer Isambard Kingdom Brunel. This famous engineer also designed the S.S. Great Britain, the Clifton Suspension Bridge and the Royal Albert Bridge at Saltash. London Paddington is famous for its association with *Paddington Bear* and there is a statue of him on Platform 1. There is also the *Paddington Bear Shop* on and *Paddington Bear Café* on the Lawn. Between Platforms 8 and 9 there is a statue of Isambard Kingdom Brunel. On Armistice Day 1922, a memorial to the employees of the GWR who died during the First World War was unveiled by Viscount Churchill. The bronze memorial, depicting a soldier reading a letter, was sculpted by Charles Sargeant Jagger and stands on platform 1. London Paddington is home to the *Great Western Railway Paddington Band*, the last railway band in England. It plays on Friday evenings on the main concourse. The concourse of the station is called "The Lawn". The former goods depot can be seen on the right as trains leave the station. This is now redeveloped as Paddington Waterside and links the station with the canalside of the *Grand Union Canal*.

In its heyday and even today, London Paddington was the "Gateway to the West" and the starting point for journeys to the Thames Valley, West Country, the Cotswolds and South Wales. The station is fronted by the magnificent former Great Western Royal Hotel, which remains a prestigious hotel known as the *Hilton London Paddington*. In its heyday London Paddington was the starting point for such famous expresses as the Cornish Riviera Express, the Royal Duchy, the Torbay Express, the Bristolian, the Red Dragon, the Pembroke Coast Express, the Cathedrals Express, the Inter-City and the Cambrian Coast Express. From 1998 London Paddington also became the gateway to the world's busiest airport when it became the terminus of the *Heathrow Express* service to London Heathrow Airport. Today London Paddington is operated by Network Rail as one of its 20 *Major Stations*.

HEATHROW EXPRESS:

The Heathrow Express is one of London's four Airport Express services along with the Gatwick Express, Stansted Express and Luton Airport Express.

It was launched in 1998 with the opening of the new rail link between London Paddington and London Heathrow Airport. The express service is operated by Heathrow Airport in partnership with Great Western Railway and takes 15 minutes. At London Paddington the services tend to use the dedicated Platforms 6 and 7. There are two stops at Heathrow: Heathrow Central, serving Terminals 2 and 3 and Heathrow Terminal 5. Until the opening of Terminal 5 on 27 March 2008, the Heathrow Express terminated at Heathrow Terminal 4. In 2010, Heathrow Express introduced a dedicated shuttle between Heathrow Central and Terminal 4.

Website: www.heathrowexpress.com

TFL ELIZABETH LINE:

The Elizabeth line stretches more than 100km from Reading and Heathrow in the west through central tunnels across to Shenfield and Abbey Wood in the east.

Detailed plans for what became the Elizabeth line started in earnest in 2001. Under an agreement between Transport for London (TfL) and the Department for Transport, the project organisation Crossrail Limited was created as a subsidiary of TfL in December 2008.

In February 2016 Queen Elizabeth II unveiled the new roundel for the Elizabeth line. A new moquette seating pattern was designed by Wallace Sewell for use on the line. The purple colour of the line and logo is reflected in the pattern.

Train services on the Elizabeth Line launched in various phases until the full line opened in 2022. TfL Rail services opened between London Liverpool Street and Shenfield May 2015 to form what would become the eastern branch of the Elizabeth line. In 2018 services to the west of London begin running as TfL Rail between London Paddington and Heathrow Airport, replacing the existing Heathrow Connect service and part of the Great Western inner suburban service. In 2019 services started between London Paddington and Reading. Finally Queen Elizabeth II formally opened the line on 18 May 2022. Elizabeth line services started on Tuesday 24 May 2022, with 10 stations under central London.

The Elizabeth line is London's first accessible railway. It is the result of the biggest infrastructure project in a generation and, as a concept, can trace its history back over a century. The Elizabeth line runs through London's first new deep tube tunnels in the 21st century. The new line connects the mainline stations at London Paddington and London Liverpool Street with Heathrow Airport and Reading in the west, and with Shenfield and Abbey Wood in the east. It increases central London's rail capacity by 10%, taking pressure off some of London Underground's busiest interchanges. The Elizabeth line is unique on the London Underground in that surface stock trains (Aventra trains built by Bombardier in Derby) run in tube tunnels under the Capital, and far out into Berkshire and Essex on the surface.

A new depot at Old Oak Common houses and maintains 42 of the Elizabeth line's 70 new trains at a time and includes many novel features. The building incorporates heating and cooling from ground sources, with solar panels and rainwater harvesting to wash trains. An automatic system scans trains as they enter, reducing the overall time needed for maintenance.

Website: https://tfl.gov.uk/modes/elizabeth-line/

Throughout this "Through the Window" guide we describe views as being left or right from the train facing in the direction of travel out of London.

London Paddington to Reading:

On leaving **London Paddington**, the train follows the elevated M40 motorway seen on the right briefly before emerging into an area of high rise development. **Royal Oak** station and **Westbourne Park** station are passed within a few minutes of departure from Paddington. Kensal Green cemetery and Old Oak Common train depot are passed to the right, while to the left can be seen the pinnacles of Wormwood Scrubs. Kensal Green cemetery is where Thackeray, Leigh Hunt, Isambard Kingdom Brunel and other famous people are buried. Wormwood Scrubs is the big prison. The prison was originally built by convict labour and houses 1400 prisoners. During the First World War, however, Wormwood Scrubs was an important airfield for the RAF. To the left as you pass the Old Oak Common train depot can be seen North Pole Depot which was built for the maintenance of the Eurostar trains through the Channel Tunnel.

This area is also the proposed location for the new **Old Oak Common** station which will be a new transport superhub in West London linking the Great Western Main Line to the new HS2 high speed line between London Euston and Birmingham Curzon Street (due to open in the early 2030s) offering quick, reliable, and comfortable journeys to the Midlands, the North and Scotland.

The former industrial area around Old Oak and Park Royal is set to be one of the largest regeneration sites in the UK. Plans to transform the wider area around the station are led by the Mayor of London's Old Oak and Park Royal Development Corporation (OPDC). Over 100 acres has been marked for development and there are plans to create 25,000 new homes and 56,000 new jobs in the area.

Next Acton Main Line station is passed through. London Underground trains share the route for much of the way to Ealing Broadway and then the surroundings become more suburban.

Beyond **West Ealing**, the Greenford branch diverges off to the right via a triangular junction and Hanwell Recreation Ground can be seen on the right, and beyond **Hanwell & Elthorne** station the tower of Hanwell Church can be seen on the right. In its churchyard lies Jonas Hanway, the man who introduced the umbrella to Britain in 1750. Soon the line is carried high over the River Brent on the 8 arched Warncliffe Viaduct built in 1837. Soon **Southall** is reached and to the left can be seen the Southall Locomotive Depot which is now used as the London base for [West Coast Railways](#) and Jeremy Hosking's [Locomotive Services TOC Ltd](#). Just beyond Southall the line crosses the [Grand Junction Canal](#) and soon **Hayes & Harlington** is reached. After **West Drayton** station the River Colne is crossed. Shortly after this the line to Heathrow Airport can be seen diverging from the mainline via a flyover to the left. Then **Iver** station is reached. The [Grand Junction Canal](#) soon draws up close to the line on the right just as **Langley** station is reached.

The French style, domed station at **Slough** dates from 1838 in parts. Here the branch line to Windsor & Eton Central can be seen branching off to the left soon after the station. Before this branch line was opened in 1850 Queen Victoria used Slough station when she travelled to Windsor Castle. The River Thames divides Windsor from its close but no less famous neighbour Eton. After leaving Slough a number of interesting factories line the route, notably the impressive brick former home of [Horlicks](#) to the right at the iconic

Horlicks Factory. This was built in 1908 and finally closed in 2018. The iconic [Horlicks Factory](#) is now being regenerated as apartments by Berkeley Group.

> **FUN FACT: DID YOU KNOW THAT…..**
>
> Slough Trading Estate, founded in 1925, is the largest industrial estate in single private ownership in Europe with over 17,000 jobs in 400 businesses.

After Slough the landscape becomes more rural, while to the left can be seen the continuous stream of planes on their final approach to London Heathrow airport. Soon **Burnham** station is passed and then **Taplow**. To the right is Taplow's 1912 church with its distinctive green spire, and then the train makes its first crossing of the River Thames. Maidenhead Bridge with its two graceful shallow brick arches spanning the river is one of Brunel's masterpieces. Opened in 1837, it confounded its critics, who firmly believed that such flat arches would surely collapse. The bridge also features in J.M.W. Turner's famous painting, *Rain, Steam and Speed*. Maidenhead still retains echoes of its Edwardian charm by the river.

Maidenhead station is where the [Bourne End and Marlow Branch](#) (often nicknamed as the Marlow Donkey) can be seen branching off to the right.

To the right of the line after **Twyford** station, where the Regatta Line branch to Henley on Thames can be seen joining the mainline on the right, are the lakes and flooded gravel pits that surround the River Loddon, a River Thames tributary. A deep cutting, the Sonning Cutting, south of Sonning then takes the line towards Reading. The railway enters the town with the River Thames right next to the line on the right hand side. To the right can be seen the white façade of [Caversham Park](#), a 1850s mansion that housed [BBC Monitoring](#) from 1943 to 2018. In 2018 it was sold by the BBC to [Beechcroft Developments](#) and converted into retirement village. Before it arrives at Reading station, the line crosses the River Kennet, the River Thames' link with the Kennet & Avon Canal and the recently reopened waterway route to Bath and Bristol. On the left the great gas holders are passed. Also the line from London Waterloo can be seen on the left as the train enters **Reading** station.

Reading is a thriving university town and shopping and business centre. Reading still has a good variety of 19th century architecture, notably the Royal Berkshire Hospital of 1837 and the 1870s municipal buildings by Waterhouse. The ruins of the Cluniac abbey, founded by King Henry I in the 12th century, underline the town's historic importance. Reading dates from the 8th century. It was an important trading and ecclesiastical centre in the Middle Ages, the site of *Reading Abbey*, one of the largest and richest monasteries of medieval England with strong royal connections, of which the 12th-century abbey gateway and significant ancient ruins remain. *Reading Museum* tells the story of the town.

Reading station is an important junction with lines running to Oxford and the Midlands, the West Country and the South West via Basingstoke. Another line to London Waterloo also connects with routes to Surrey and Kent. Reading station has a gracious Italianate façade of 1870, crowned with a decorative clock tower, but however to the side is the new station complete with shopping arcade. Today Reading is operated by Network Rail as one of its 20 *Major Stations*. Outside Reading railway station is the former Great Western Hotel which is now the *Malmaison Reading*. From Reading there are regular *RailAir* express coach services to London Heathrow Airport.

FUN FACT: DID YOU KNOW THAT…..

The first restaurant of the iconic "Little Chef" restaurant chain opened in Reading in 1958. The brand was inspired by American style roadside diners. The restaurant chain was famous for the "Olympic Breakfast" – its version of a full English Breakfast – as well as its "Early Starter" and "Jubilee Pancakes". There were 12 restaurants located around England by 1965. The chain expanded rapidly throughout the 1970s, and its parent company would acquire the Happy Eater chain in the 1980s, its only major roadside competitor. When its owners converted all Happy Eater restaurants to Little Chef in the late 1990s, this allowed it to peak in scale with 439 restaurants. Sadly in the 2000s the brand started a dramatic decline and was closed in 2018.

FUN FACT: DID YOU KNOW THAT…..

Reading University was founded in 1892 as University College, Reading, a University of Oxford extension college by the University of Oxford's Christ Church College. It only gained independence from University of Oxford and received the power to grant its own degrees in 1926 by royal charter from King George V and was the only university to receive such a charter between the two world wars.

Website: https://www.reading.ac.uk/

Reading to Taunton:

On leaving **Reading** the line to the West Country leaves the mainline to Bristol, Oxford and the Midlands which can be seen heading off to the right. To the right are the fields alongside the River Thames that every year around the August Bank Holiday weekend are host to the *Reading Festival* which is one of the UK's major summer music festivals and was launched in 1971.

The train then runs past housing estates to **Reading West**, and then soon enters open country as they cross the River Kennet. The line to Basingstoke is soon seen diverging off to the left. From this point the river and the Kennet & Avon Canal are never far from the line, and the canal with its restored locks, its handsome brick bridges and its brightly painted narrow boats is an enjoyable feature of the journey. With the gravel works and lakes of the Kennet valley to the left, the line passes under the M4 and then **Theale** comes into view, marked by its large early Victorian church. The next station is **Aldermaston**, but its village with its pretty brick cottages is over a mile to the south of the station. Since 1950 it is also home to the UK Government's *Atomic Weapons Establishment (AWE)* and has become synonymous with CND (Campaign for Nuclear Disarmament) protest marches ever since. In a historic first, Britain's first roadside petrol filling station was opened by The AA on the Bath Road near Aldermaston on 2 March 1919. Closer to hand is Midgham Church, Victorian and decorative, and attractively placed in a field just to the west of **Midgham** station. At Thatcham, another station some distance from its town, there is a canal lock just to the left.

Approaching Newbury, the train passes *Newbury Racecourse* to the left, whose weather boarded station, **Newbury Racecourse**, still retains its GWR name boards. At **Newbury** station, little of the town can be seen, but the centre is not far away, easily accessible on foot.

Newbury has plenty to offer the visitor. The great 16th century church and 17th century cloth hall, which now houses a museum, reveal the town's former wealth as a centre of the wool trade. In the 15th century over 1000 wool weavers were employed here, in what was England's first true factory. Prosperity continued in later centuries, particularly after the opening of the *Kennet & Avon Canal*, which winds its way through the town centre, and the legacy is an interesting variety of buildings from all periods, including some groups of almshouses and a Victorian corn exchange. Newbury is also famous for the two Civil War battles that were fought near the town.

Leaving Newbury, the train enters a wooded stretch, with glimpses of the pretty village of Hamstead Marshall to the left as it passes the close group of the mill, the pub and the canal lock. To the right is the classical façade of 18th century Benham House, set in its Capability Brown park. **Kintbury** village is to the south of its station, clustered around its large church. After Kintbury the river valley becomes more defined and the line runs along the southern slopes with good views across to the northern side, beyond the river and the canal. **Hungerford** is a handsome town, with all its main buildings in one street which climbs southwards away from the river. From the railway bridge just west of the station, there is a clear view of the town centre to the left, with its good range of 18th and 19th century buildings, but trains approaching from the west offer the best view of the church and its vicarage, pleasantly set beside the river and the canal. West of Hungerford the line overlooks the canal and the river valley, and then it crosses the canal again near Froxfield, where the decorative gothic façade of the almshouses founded by the Duchess of Somerset in 1694 can be clearly seen.

Railway and canal now run close together to Little Bedwyn, a delightful little village with its 12th century church, its row of 1860s estate cottages, all in coloured brick, and the 18th century buildings by the canal and lock. Locks appear quite frequently now as the canal climbs towards its summit, a few miles to the south west, and the train soon reaches **Bedwyn**. Near the station is Great Bedwyn's large church with its grand central tower and pretty graveyard, and a short walk away is the attractive village.

After Bedwyn the line continues west through the rolling countryside of the Marlborough Downs. The *Kennet & Avon Canal* continues to parallel the railway to the left and the famous *Crofton Beam Engines* at Crofton Pumping Station are passed to the right and then the canal disappears into a tunnel near Savernake.

FUN FACT: DID YOU KNOW THAT…..

Crofton Pumping Station on the Kennet and Avon Canal in Wiltshire houses two working beam engines that are historic engineering masterpieces and are among the oldest beam engines in the world. The Boulton and Watt engine, built in 1812, is the oldest beam engine in the world still in its original setting and carrying out its original job. The Harvey & Co. of Hayle, Cornwall engine, built in 1846 and modified in 1905, is one of the few remaining operating engines of its type.

It is a rare survivor of the technology which enabled British engineers to drain mines and supply towns and cities with water throughout the world. It is one of the most significant industrial heritage sites in the United Kingdom and a fascinating visitor attraction that enables the visitor to step into our industrial and social history and turn back the clock to a time when steam was king.

Website: https://www.croftonbeamengines.org/

Soon the village of Woolton Rivers can be seen to the right as the line draws alongside Martinsell Hill. The summit of which is crowned by a large prehistoric camp covering more than 30 acres. The hill rises 947 ft high and commands fine views across Salisbury Plain which stretches away to the left of the railway line.

Soon the line reaches **Pewsey** station with its village to the left, with its church rising above the village. Salisbury Plain continues to stretch away to the left. To the right can be seen Picked Hill and Woodborough Hill. Due north from here lies the ancient site of [Avebury](#) one of the many ancient sites that lie alongside this route to the west. To the right also can be seen Milk Hill and its famous [Pewsey White Horse](#). This horse only dates from 1812 but some of the other white horses in this part of the country are very ancient including the Westbury White Horse which the line passes later on in the journey. Then to the right can be seen the village of Woodborough. The ancient earthwork of Rybury Camp can be seen to the right. While to the left is the village of Beechingstoke and the vast expanse of Salisbury Plain stretching away to the south. Then a broad valley opens up to the right and the line bends south west. The village of Potterne can be seen to the right, and on the left the village of Great Cheverell appears. Also to the left the long line of Salisbury Plain forms the horizon. Coulston Hill and Stoke Hill are seen as a background to the village of East Coulston while a little further on Edington Hill can be seen behind the village of Edington. This village has the beautiful Priory Church at its heart. This splendid piece of 14th century architecture was built by William de Edyndune, who became Bishop of Winchester and began the important rebuilding of Winchester Cathedral which was completed by his successor William of Wykeham.

The next hill viewed to the left is Westbury Hill and at the summit can be seen the great earthwork of [Bratton Camp](#) with fine trenches clearly marked by the long ridges on the hillside. Legend tells that it was at this spot that the Danish King Guthrum retired after suffering a heavy defeat by King Alfred the Great at the Battle of Ethandune in 878.

Westbury Hill juts out prominently from the main form of Salisbury Plain at this point and soon another famous landmark comes into view on its western slopes. This is the famous [Westbury White Horse](#). Unlike its counterpart we saw earlier in the journey at Milk Hill near Pewsey, this White Horse is very ancient. Legend tells how it may have been cut to commemorate King Alfred the Great's great victory over King Guthrum. But having become overgrown in places it was recut in 1778 and received further attention in 1873. It measures 175 ft from head to tail and stands 107 ft high.

Soon the Westbury avoiding line can be seen diverging off to the left and if the train is not stopping at Westbury then it will take the avoiding line and the town can be seen to the left. However if the train is calling at Westbury station then it will continue and the line from Bristol can be seen joining the mainline from the right. Then the train enters **Westbury** station. This station is an important junction for trains to Bristol and Salisbury.

After leaving Westbury the line to Salisbury can be seen diverging to the left and soon the Westbury avoiding line rejoins the mainline from the left. Away to the left can be seen Cley Hill rising in the distance. Like many high hills in this part of England it too has a prehistoric camp at the summit. The hill rises to 800 ft and commands fine views. Historically it is of interest as it was one of the sites chosen for the great beacon fires that gave warning of the approach of the Spanish Armada. Soon the valley of the Frome is reached. Again Frome station, like Westbury, has an avoiding line to allow express trains to bypass the station. This is soon seen diverging off to the left. Just before entering **Frome** station the disused line to Radstock can be seen joining the mainline from the right. After leaving Frome the avoiding line rejoins from the left and the journey continues westwards.

Cley Hill continues to keep the line company after Frome and the hill could be considered as the western outpost of Salisbury Plain as soon we enter a different landscape. The change is marked almost at once by the fine mass of woodland around _Longleat House_, the ancestral home of the Most Hon. The Marquess of Bath. The house stands beside a beautiful lake in a widespread deer park, hidden from view by the beautiful Longleat Woods to the left.

LONGLEAT HOUSE

Longleat House is widely regarded as one of the finest examples of Elizabethan architecture in Britain. It is the ancestral home of the Marquesses of Bath. In 1949 Longleat House became the first stately home in Britain to be opened to the public on a commercial basis. Longleat Safari Park opened in 1966 as the first drive-through safari park outside Africa, and is home to over 500 animals, including giraffe, monkeys, rhino, lion, tigers and wolves. Today you can see their amazing animals by car, foot, train, bus and boat. The 9,800-acre estate, of which the park occupies 900 acres, has long been one of the top British tourist attractions, and has motivated other large landowners to generate income from their heritage too.

Website: https://www.longleat.co.uk/

To the right spreads Postlebury Wood over Postlebury hill. These woodlands form part of Witham Park. Soon the village of Witham Friary is passed. Here the line to the Cranmore and now home of the [East Somerset Railway](#) diverges from the mainline to the right. Soon the village of Upton Noble lies to the right.

EAST SOMERSET RAILWAY:

The East Somerset Railway is a heritage steam railway that operates between Cranmore and Mendip Vale through the beautiful Mendip countryside. It has a mainline connection but this section is used by freight trains to the Merehead Quarry. The heritage railway was founded by David Shepherd, the famous wildlife artist and conservationist, in 1971. At Cranmore station you can explore the David Shepherd Discovery Centre which celebrates the history of the railway and the life of the world famous wildlife artist whose vision for the railway made it what it is today.

Website: https://eastsomersetrailway.com/

The little River Brue now flows beside the line on the left, and soon the little town of **Bruton** is reached. On the right the land slopes down gently into the valley of the Brue and its tributary, the River Alham, we have a view of the distant Mendip Hills. Soon the ancient town of Castle Cary lies to the left and **Castle Cary** station is reached. This is close to where the [Glastonbury Festival](#) is held at Worthy Farm and is one of the world's most legendary music festivals. Just after the station the line to Yeovil, Dorchester and Weymouth diverges left from the mainline.

GLASTONBURY FESTIVAL:

The Glastonbury Festival is the UK's greatest music festival and was founded by Michael Eavis in 1970 and is held most years at Worthy Farm. It is the largest green space open air music and performing arts festival in the world and a template for all the festivals that have come after it. The festival takes place in a beautiful location – 900 acres in the Vale of Avalon, an area steeped in symbolism, mythology and religious traditions dating back many hundreds of years overlooked by Glastonbury Tor and with stunning views across the Somerset Levels. Over the decades it has gained an iconic and legendary status in the event calendar and is attended by around 175,000 people and is broadcast on TV too. In 2014, the V&A Museum acquired guardianship of the Glastonbury Festival Archive, an eclectic and growing resource that reveals how the Festival has developed over the past 50 years to become the global cultural phenomenon that it is today. It is famed for the iconic Pyramid Stage and sells out in minutes, and has hosted many of music's most important and high-profile performers since its inception in 1970.

Website: https://www.glastonburyfestivals.co.uk/

A striking landmark that can be seen to the right, looking west, is Glastonbury Tor, a prominent hill with the ruined chapel of St Michael on its summit. Soon on the left can be seen the church tower of Lovington. While also on the left in the distance can be seen Cadbury Castle. Around the steep sides of the hill are four lines of earthworks and this camp is said to have been the last British stronghold in the West to hold out against the Romans. Wheathill Church stands close to the line on the left, and East Lydford Church on the right, with Glastonbury Tor still visible in the distance.

Next is the village of Keinton Mandeville on the right. This village is the birthplace of Sir Henry Irving in 1838. He was a famous actor in the Victorian era and inspiration for Dracula. Pennard Hill near Glastonbury rises up 400 ft on the right. While on the left is the village of Charlton Adam and its church tower. Then Charlton Mackrell is passed on the right. To the right appears Dundon Hill beyond Copley Wood. Soon we reach Somerton. It is a picturesque little place with an ancient market cross and other old buildings. It stands of the River Cary. After passing Somerton the railway enters Somerton Tunnel, and it is the first tunnel after leaving London. After the tunnel the small market town of Langport is passed. This town lies on the River Parrett. Hills rise either side of the railway here, but the valley of the Parrett broadens out into another expanse of low lying country. The stretch lying immediately to the right is Aller Moor and where the hills subside into the valley is the village of Aller. This is where King Alfred the Great is said to have baptised King Guthrun and many of his followers in the Saxon font which can still be seen in Aller Church soon after the battle of Ethandune. Away to the right beyond the villages of Othery and Middlezoy stretches Sedgemoor, famous for the site of the battle of Sedgemoor which ended the Duke of Monmouth's rebellion in 1685.

The Polden Hills can be seen rising beyond the level stretch of Sedgemoor, while to the left on the higher ground bordering West Sedge Moor is seen the Parkfield Monument, erected in 1768 by the Earl of Chatham to commemorate Sir William Pynsent. Also on the left is the village of Stoke St Gregory. To the right can be seen the great Burrow Bridge Mound, identified by legend as 'King Alfred's Fort', and actually used as a fort during the Civil Wars. Athelney is close to the junction of the River Tone and River Parrett. Soon the line passes the Isle of Athelney to the left and the legendary location of the humble cottage where King Alfred the Great had his telling off after burning the cakes! Here in these marshes he took refuge and rested while preparing the final assault against the Danes. The Isle is a slight rise above the level of the flat lands; and in medieval times there was an abbey, but now there is a pillar erected in 1801, with an inscription commemorating King Alfred the Great. Looking ahead to the right a distant view can be seen of the Quantock Hills. A little way beyond the Isle of Athelney to the right can be seen the village of Lyng. While on the left beyond the level stretch of Curry Moor, through which flows the River Tone, is seen the village of North Curry. In the distance are the Blackdown Hills.

Soon the line joins the mainline from Bristol to Taunton via a flyover and the *Bridgewater & Taunton Canal* can be seen on the right. While on the left the River Tone follows the line past the village of Creech St Michael whose church is famous for the extremely ancient carving of the Holy Trinity above the west door. The neighbouring village of Ruishton also presents an ancient church with a fine tower. The M5 soon crosses the railway and then **Taunton** station is reached.

Taunton is a fine town with a rich history. *Taunton Castle* (now home to the Museum of Somerset and the *Castle Hotel*) was founded in the 8th century by King Ina, King of the West Saxons, and a large part of the medieval building still remains. Taunton also played an important role in the English Civil War and was chosen by the Duke of Monmouth as the place where he proclaimed himself King. An event which had its sequel in the Bloody Assize held here by Judge Jeffreys.

FUN FACT: DID YOU KNOW THAT…..

Taunton in Somerset was the first town in the UK to be lit permanently by electric street lighting in 1881. This was 12 months before the Electric Lighting Act of 1882 which enforced the switch from oil lamps to electric across the UK.

FUN FACT: DID YOU KNOW THAT…..

The West Country including Somerset (along with Devon, Herefordshire, Gloucestershire and Worcestershire) is famed for its orchards and is a major cider producing area. There are more than 400 different varieties of cider apple grown in Somerset alone, which is enough to keep the keenest scrumper busy. Indeed, England consumes more cider per capita than any other country in the world and is the largest producer of cider in Europe.

FUN FACT: DID YOU KNOW THAT…..

Ten pin bowling has its origins in the game of Somerset skittles, that was played on outside lawns with nine wooden pins. Today ten pin bowling is mainly played in indoor bowling alleys and remains a popular game.

FUN FACT: DID YOU KNOW THAT…..

The 'Frome Hoard' is the largest collection of Roman coins ever found in a single container and can now be seen in the Museum of Somerset at Taunton.

Taunton to Exeter St Davids:

Soon after leaving Taunton a view across to the Blackdown Hills opens out to the left and the Wellington obelisk is seen on the ridge. On the right is seen *Taunton School*, a notable public school, located at Staplegrove. The school opened its history in 1847 as the Independent College, a centre of education for boys from nonconformist families. The buildings date from 1870.

The ancient octagonal church tower on the left is that of Bishop's Hull. To the right is the village of Norton Fitzwarren and site of **Norton Fitzwarren** station is soon reached. This station was where the branches to Barnstaple and Minehead diverged off to the right. Sadly only the Minehead line now remains and is home to the *West Somerset Railway*. On the left the village of Bradford on Tone appears.

WEST SOMERSET RAILWAY:

The West Somerset Railway is a heritage steam railway that offers 20 miles of heritage railway through stunning Somerset countryside and coast. It operates regular services between Minehead and Bishop's Lydeard, near Taunton. It is the longest independent railway in Britain. The line meanders through the Quantock Hills, an area of outstanding natural beauty and along the Bristol Channel Coast. . It has a mainline connection which is used by occasional through excursion trains.

Website: https://www.west-somerset-railway.co.uk/

The Blackdown Hills and the *Wellington Monument* come into closer view as we head south west. Then the town of Wellington is passed. There are two Wellingtons – one in Somerset and one in Shropshire. However it is this Somerset Wellington that gives the great Iron Duke and the Duke of Wellington their title. Again to the left can be seen the Wellington Monument erected in honour of the Battle of Waterloo and the Duke of Wellington's victory. Wellington is also home to the notable public school, *Wellington School*. Soon the village of Sampford Arundel is passed to the left and Culmstock Beacon can be seen on the western end of the Blackdown Hills. After this the landscape slopes down into the Culm Valley.

FUN FACT: DID YOU KNOW THAT…..

It was while descending Wellington Bank in Somerset in 1904 with an Ocean Mails boat train from Plymouth to London Paddington that GWR No 3440 City of Truro steam locomotive found its place in history and broke a speed record. On 9th May 1904 City of Truro achieved a speed of 102.3mph on the descent of Wellington Bank between Exeter and Taunton. It was not only the first locomotive to reach and pass the magical speed of 100mph, but the first vehicle of any kind to reach such a milestone. This gave it iconic and legendary status and as a result it is now preserved as part of the National Railway Museum collection and is on static display at the STEAM Museum of the Great Western Railway in Swindon.

FUN FACT: DID YOU KNOW THAT…..

The countryside around Tiverton is famed for its dairy farming and in the 1920s and 30s it was here that the concept of Young Farmers Clubs was founded starting with the Culm Valley Young Farmers Club and the national network that is the National Federation of Young Farmers Clubs. Today it is one of the largest rural youth organisations in the UK and is dedicated to young people who have a love for agriculture and rural life.

Website: https://www.nfyfc.org.uk

At this point the train has started the ascent of Wellington Bank which is a steep gradient and soon enters Whiteball Tunnel. Soon the village of Burlescombe is seen on the left and behind it is the M5 motorway which soon runs alongside the railway. To the right is the Grand Western Canal. This connects the River Tone with the River Exe which the canal enters at Tiverton. Soon the village of Sampford Peverel is seen to the right and **Tiverton Parkway** station is reached alongside the M5 motorway.

After leaving Tiverton Parkway to the north west on the right of the line can be seen Barton Hill. To the left across the Culm Valley is the village of Kentisbeare. Soon the village of Willand is passed. The Culm River is an important tributary of the River Exe, coming down from the southern slopes of the Blackdown Hills. Soon the next settlement passed is Cullompton. All the way the M5 parallels the railway line to the left. The railway then crosses the River Culm and to the right appears the village of Bradninch. Bradninch was a chartered borough as long ago as 1208 and from the time of King Edward II to that of King Henry VII returned two Members of Parliament. Bradninch Manor House which stands to the right on the outskirts of the village, is one of the finest examples of an Elizabethan interior in the country. Some of the rooms are finely carved and panelled. King Charles I stayed at the old Rectory during the Civil War.

The wooded hill which rises prominently close to the railway on the left is Dolbury Hill. Rising sharply out of the landscape by Killerton Park it checks the River Culm on its course and forces it to make a wide detour. The M5 motorway also disappears from view behind the hill. Soon the River Culm can be seen again on the left and from the right it is joined by the River Exe. The village of Rewe is passed by close to the railway on the left. Then again on the left the village of Stoke Canon is passed. Then across the River Exe can be seen the village of Brampford Speke. Just after Stoke Canon the River Exe passes under the railway to join the River Culm with the beautiful Stoke Woods rising up to the right.

The River Exe is a beautiful and interesting river, beginning its story way up in the hills and rocky tors of Exmoor. It rises in the centre of Exmoor Forest only a few miles from the North Devon coast but heads across Devon to find its way into the sea on the South Devon coast at Exmouth. At Tiverton it receives the River Lowman, made famous by Blackmore in the 'Lorna Doone'.

Soon the railway heads down into the historic city of Exeter. At Cowley Bridge the [Tarka Valley Line](#) (one of the [Great Scenic Railways of Devon & Cornwall](#)) from Barnstaple can be seen joining the mainline from the right. The [Dartmoor Line](#) (one of the [Great Scenic Railways of Devon & Cornwall](#)) from Okehampton also joins. As we approach Exeter the city spreads itself out on the hill to the left and soon **Exeter St Davids** station is reached.

> **FUN FACT: DID YOU KNOW THAT…..**
>
> In 1934 Sir Allen Lane famously got inspiration for creation of [Penguin Books](#) while waiting for a train at Exeter St Davids. Penguin Books famously transformed publishing industry with its affordable paperbacks that brought books to the masses. In April 2023 a Penguin Books vending machine was installed at Exeter St Davids rail station in the main entrance hall by a partnership of Penguin Books, Exeter UNESCO City of Literature and Great Western Railway. This book vending machine will allow passengers to buy a wide range of Penguin Books.

Exeter was a fortified town and a busy port from the Roman period onwards, but it was the Normans who developed the city as it stands today. Their legacy is the great [Exeter Cathedral](#) with its flanking Norman towers. Greatly expanded during the Middle Ages, the cathedral is also known for its vaulting and 14th century sculptures in the west front. It was the River Exe and the port that made Exeter a wealthy city in the Middle Ages and the surviving timber framed buildings reflect this. In order to maintain its wealth, the city built its ship canal to the sea, from 1564. Exeter today is a thriving city with an exciting past. Indeed Exeter is one of the oldest cities in the West Country as always been a capital in a wider sense than being the county town of Devon. Its position here in the West Country is similar to that of Winchester to the ancient kingdom of Wessex. Exeter is also a bustling commercial city and a great railway centre. At Exeter there is the [Dartmoor Explorer](#) bus service to Plymouth via Moretonhampstead, Princetown and Yelverton across Dartmoor. There are regular bus services from Exeter St Davids to Exeter Airport.

Here at Exeter St Davids the former Southern Railway line from London Waterloo joins the Great Western mainline. In its heyday Southern Railway expresses from Waterloo crossed with Great Western ones from Paddington each heading in opposite directions. Southern ones going north via Okehampton and down into Plymouth via Tavistock, while Great Western ones went south via the famous sea wall section at Dawlish to Plymouth. Sadly today only the Great Western route survives as a through mainline.

Exeter St Davids to Paignton:

Shortly after leaving **Exeter St Davids** station the line to London Waterloo diverges from the mainline to the left and heads up the steep Exeter Incline to Exeter Central station. The line from Exeter St Davids and Exeter Central east towards London Waterloo is known as the [East Devon Line](#) as far as Axminster (one of the [Great Scenic Railways of Devon & Cornwall](#)). There is also the [Avocet Line](#) to Exmouth (one of the [Great Scenic Railways of Devon & Cornwall](#)).

As our train leaves Exeter and heads westwards we pass **Exeter St Thomas** station and a view of the magnificent [Exeter Cathedral](#) and the city opens up to the left. We then pass the new rail station at **Marsh Barton** that opened on 4 July 2023. This station serves Exeter's largest industrial estate and is in close proximity to the Riverside Valley Park which offers wonderful routes for walking and cycling alongside the River Exe. It also helps connect to the Royal Devon & Exeter Hospital.

The following section of railway round to Plymouth is one of the most famous sections of railway in the world and is very scenic as it follows the legendary Dawlish sea wall section and then at Teignmouth turns inland and over the South Devon banks to Plymouth. The section from Exeter St Davids along the Dawlish sea wall to Newton Abbot and on to Paignton is known as the [Riviera Line](#) (one of the [Great Scenic Railways of Devon & Cornwall](#)). Here the River Exe is on our left, but the waterway nearest the railway is the Exeter Canal. This canal runs between the railway and the River Exe for about 5 miles. It was one of the first canals built in England, having been commenced in Queen Elizabeth I's time. Soon to the right the pinnacled tower of Alphington Church is visible. While to the left the ancient seaport of Topsham can be seen across the River Exe.

This is on the Exeter Central to Exmouth railway line. This line can be seen from time to time following the river bank on the other side of the River Exe. On the right is the village of Exminster with a 15th century church containing one of the ornate Devonshire carved screens.

Soon on the right can be seen the village of Powderham with its Church and Belvidere Tower. The Tower is set on a hill with wide views over the estuary of the River Exe. On the left across the River Exe can be seen [Nutwell Court](#). The great treasure of this house is a panel from Sir Francis Drake's ship 'The Golden Hind'. Behind can be seen the waterside village of Lympstone.

Next the focus of interest shifts to the right once more as [Powderham Castle](#). This is the ancestral home of the Right Hon. The Earl of Devon and is set in its vast deer park. The castle was built about the time of the Norman conquest and has been the home of the Courtenay family since 1377 who have been Earls of Devon since 1533.

Soon the train reaches **Starcross** station and here there is a splendid view across to Exmouth. A notable feature of Starcross is the Italianate pumping engine house which can be seen to the right as we pass Starcross station. It is the best surviving building from Brunel's unsuccessful Atmospheric Railway. This abortive enterprise is commemorated in the "Atmospheric Railway" pub located opposite the railway station. The engine house is now home to the Starcross Sailing & Cruising Club. From Starcross there is a ferry service to Exmouth operated by *Starcross Exmouth Ferry*. Between here and Exmouth is the vast open stretch of water that is the estuary of the River Exe. Also there is Dawlish Warren a sandbank which thrusts itself out into the Exe like a breakwater at the mouth of the river. At the western end of it is **Dawlish Warren** station, with Langstone Cliff rising up just beyond. Here the railway runs alongside the sea wall and the open sea for the first time. A fine headland that rises on the opposite side of the estuary beyond Exmouth hides from view the seaside town of Budleigh Salterton which lurks just round the corner. Near the station is *Brunel Holiday Park* where five railway carriages are camping coaches.

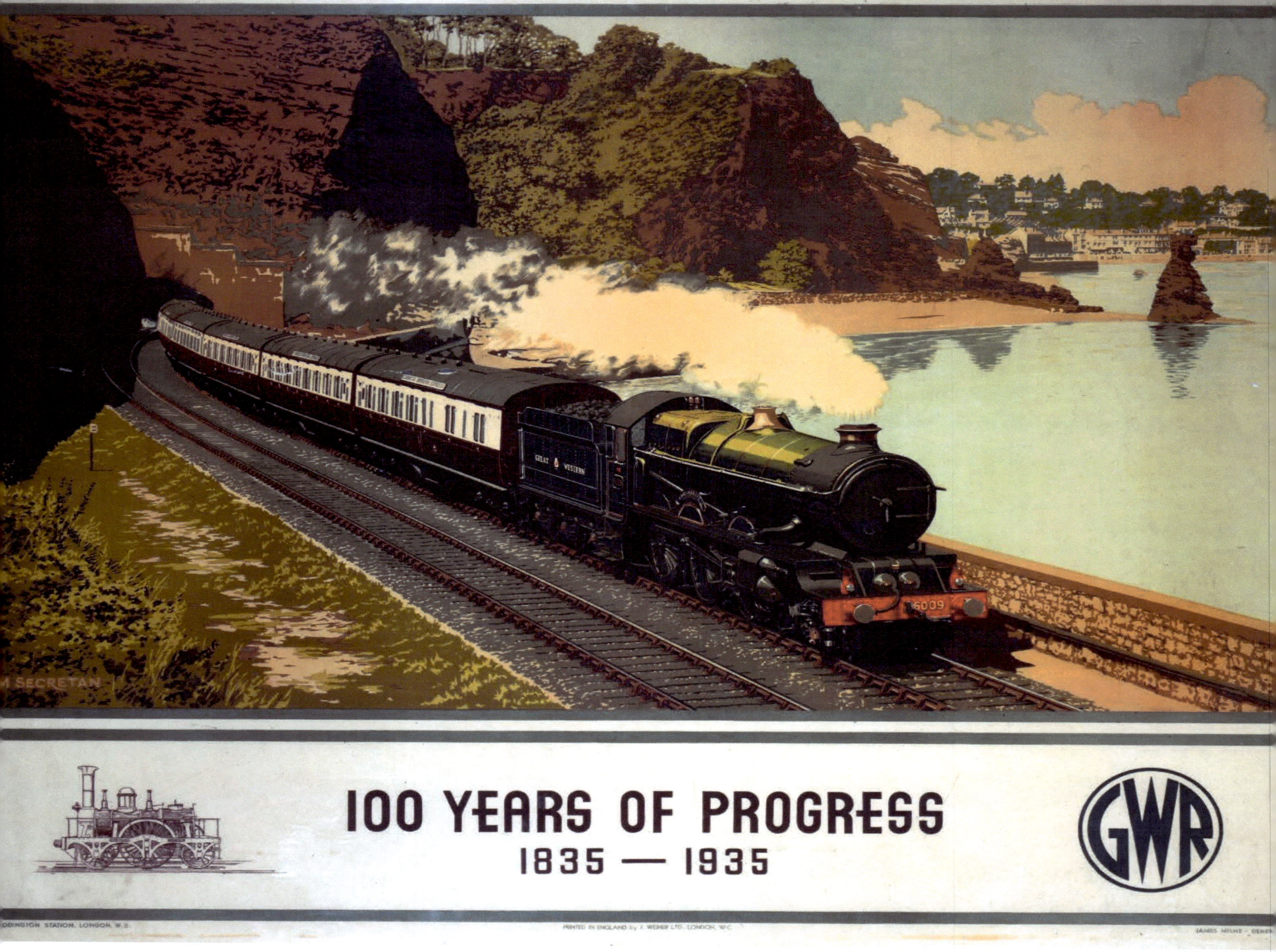

 100 YEARS OF PROGRESS
1835 — 1935

Fine red sandstone cliffs rise up on the right as the railway runs alongside the famous Great Western sea wall which continues all the way to Teignmouth. However the next station reached is **Dawlish** and this is the first seaside resort reached on the Cornish Riviera route from London. Dawlish is divided into two distinct parts, the old town on the right with Dawlish Water running through it and the new town. The next section of the line along the famous sea wall is punctuated by the train plunging into tunnels at regular intervals with glimpses of the sea in between. The first tunnel reached is Kennaway Tunnel followed by Phillot Tunnel. Next follows Clerk's Tunnel and then Coryton Tunnel. This is the namesake to Coryton Cove one of the small coves along this stretch of coast. Finally comes Parson's Tunnel the longest and last of the series. On our exit to the left can be seen the Parson & Clerk Rock. If we look back the way we have come at this point we will see the wide expanse of sea to where the Devon coast runs into Dorset in the east and on a fine day you can see all the way to Portland Bill. Today this section of coast is known as the [Jurassic Coast - the Dorset & East Devon Coast World Heritage Site](). Beyond Parson's Tunnel the line reaches the outskirts of Teignmouth a highly picturesque seaside resort and port at the mouth of the River Teign. The Danes raided it hundreds of years ago as did the French in1690. Here the railway turns inland after a brief glimpse of the seafront and reaches **Teignmouth** station.

After Teignmouth the line follows the River Teign inland and passes the [Port of Teignmouth]() before running inland alongside the River Teign. Across the estuary to the left can be seen the village of Shaldon which lies at the waterside in the shadow of Ness Rock. Soon we can see the Teignmouth Bridge which carries the road from Teignmouth to Torquay across the estuary of the River Teign. The village of Bishop's Teignton can be seen on the right had an ancient importance through its close association with the Bishops of Exeter who had a country residence here. The Little Haldon Hills which spread inland from here are the foothills to the vast expanse of Dartmoor. Soon the line passes King's Teignton on the right and across the country to the right can be seen one of the famous Dartmoor tors, Haytor, which is 1,400 ft high and is crowned by a magnificent heap of rocks. Next the railway passes under the A380 main road and [Newton Abbot Racecourse]() is passed on the right and a moment later **Newton Abbot** station is reached. Just after the Racecourse is passed the disused former branch line to Heathfield and Moretonhampstead joins the mainline on the right. Near Moretonhampstead was the former Great Western Railway owned hotel [Manor House Hotel (now the Bovey Castle Hotel)](). Newton Abbot is a pleasant town at the head of the Teign estuary and is an important junction for connections to the English Riviera at Torquay and Paignton and it also is a good centre for visiting the [Dartmoor National Park]().

After Newton Abbot station the mainline becomes four tracks as the Riviera Line (one of the Great Scenic Railways of Devon & Cornwall) to Paignton separates off to the left at Aller Junction. Torquay, Paignton and Brixham, centred around Tor Bay, are known as the English Riviera and the line once continued beyond Paignton to Kingswear (for Dartmouth); however, this section of line is now home to the Dartmouth Steam Railway & Riverboat Company.

The train heads through the former station of Kingskerswell before reaching the English Riviera holiday resorts of **Torre** and **Torquay.**

On the left, as we depart Torquay station, can be seen the rear of the Grand Hotel Torquay. This is one of the top hotels on the English Riviera and has a Dame Agatha Christie connection. This is where Agatha and Archie Christie spent their honeymoon night after their wedding in Bristol on Christmas Eve, 1914. Two days later Agatha travelled up to London with her new husband and waved him goodbye as he set off for war in France. It was to be 6 months before they would see each other again and nearly four years before their married life could really begin. The Grand Hotel now has an Agatha Christie Suite. The hotel's popular restaurant and bar have fine sea views. The *Imperial Hotel* in Torquay is another top hotel on the English Riviera and was Agatha Christie's inspiration for the Majestic Hotel in the Poirot books. *Western Lady Ferries* operate between Torquay and Brixham across Tor Bay.

Soon, the train reaches **Paignton**. On this last section, through these picturesque Devon seaside towns and villages, the train rides high above the towns with magnificent views to the left across Tor Bay and the surrounding area. Notable hotels in Paignton include the *Palace Hotel*, *Redcliffe Hotel* and the *Marine Hotel*.

The Torbay Express from London Paddington is truly a gateway and holiday line to the English Riviera. Torquay, Paignton and Brixham are known as the *English Riviera* and the line continues beyond Paignton to Kingswear (for Dartmouth); however, this section of the line is now home to the *Dartmouth Steam Railway & Riverboats Company,* and their station is adjacent to Paignton station. There are occasional direct-through steam excursions from the mainline from time to time.

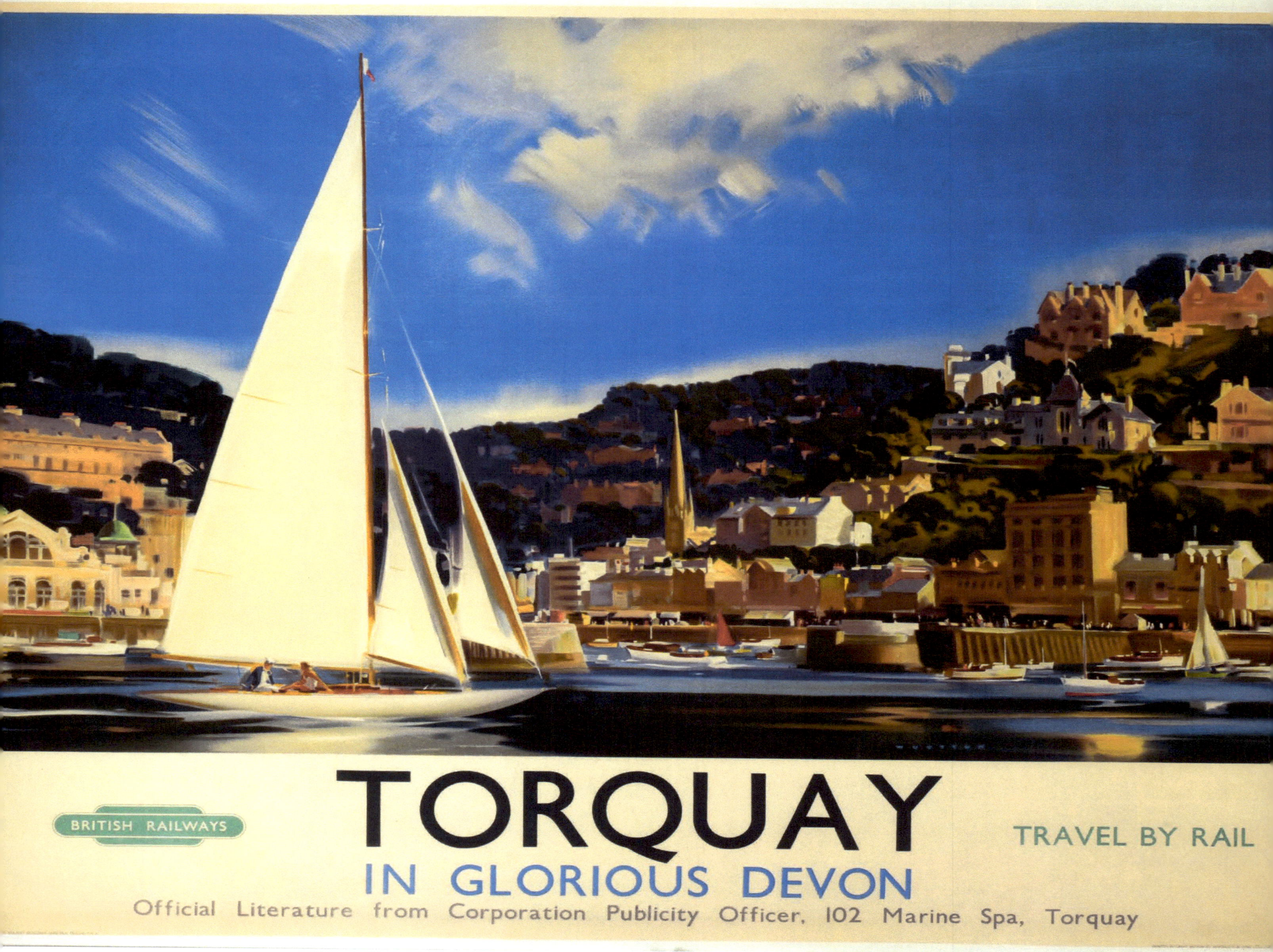

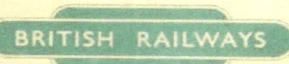

TORQUAY
IN GLORIOUS DEVON
BRITISH RAILWAYS
TRAVEL BY RAIL
Official Literature from Corporation Publicity Officer, 102 Marine Spa, Torquay

The enchanting
RIVER DART
Travel by Rail to Totnes or Dartmouth
Thence by River Dart Company's Steamers
TERN REGION

NORTH, SOUTH, EAST OR WEST,
SOUTH DEVON IS GLORIOUS
SOUTH DEVON IS BEST!
N
S
E
W
SEATON
SIDMOUTH
EXETER
EXMOUTH
CHAGFORD
DAWLISH
DARTMOOR
NEWTON ABBOT
TEIGNMOUTH
TORQUAY
BUCKFAST ABBEY
BUCKFASTLEIGH
PLYMOUTH
PAIGNTON
TOTNES
BRIXHAM
DARTMOUTH
For Holidays
this year, try –
SUNNY SOUTH DEVO
GWR
IT'S QUICKER BY RAIL
FREE GUIDEBOOK MAY BE OBTAINED FROM THE INFORMATION BUREAU AT ANY OF THE R

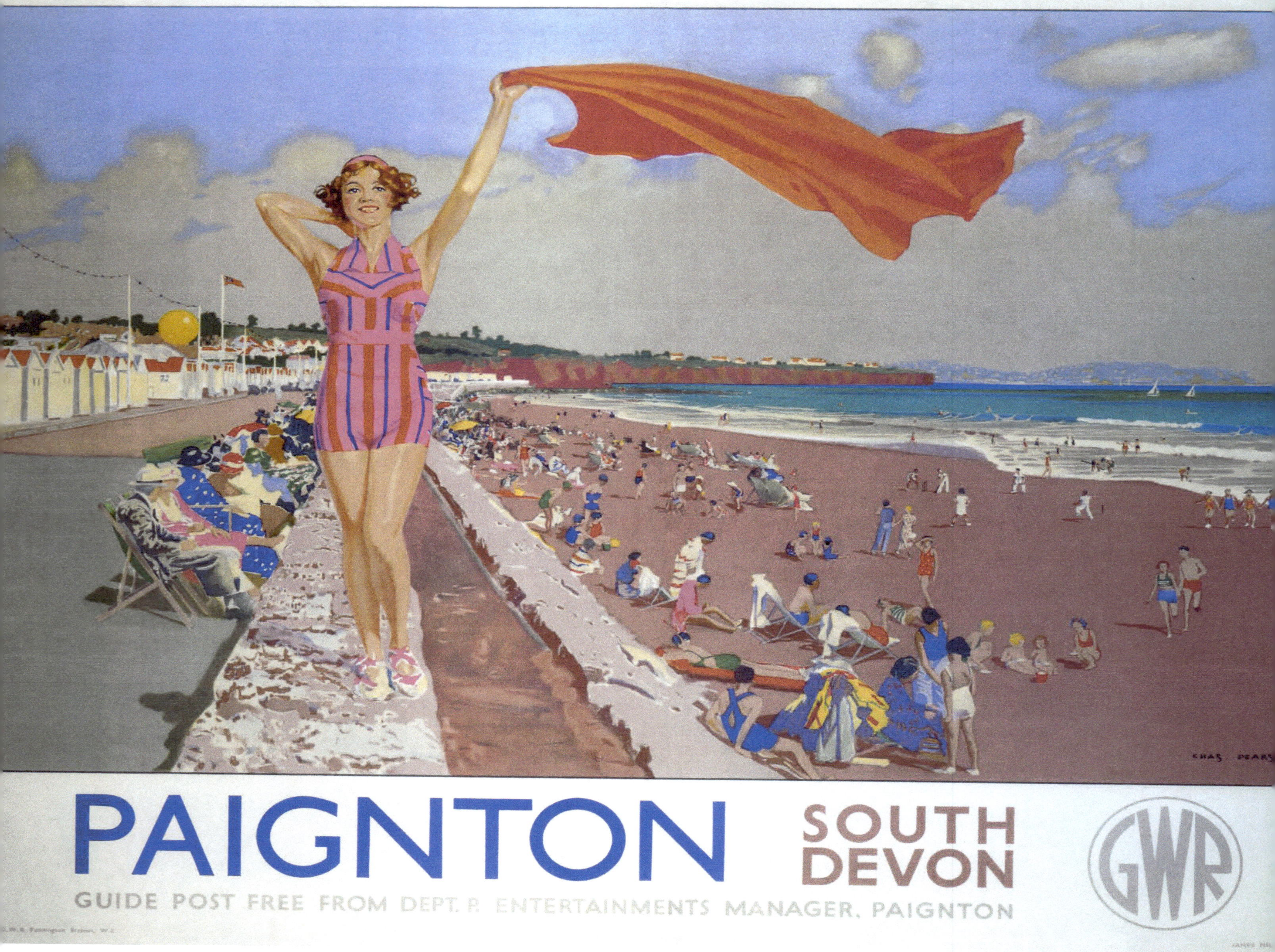
CHAS. PEARS
PAIGNTON
SOUTH
DEVON
GUIDE POST FREE FROM DEPT. P. ENTERTAINMENTS MANAGER, PAIGNTON
GWR

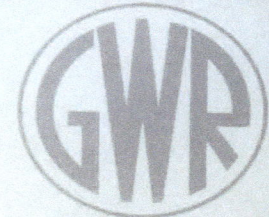

The Dartmouth Steam Railway & Riverboats Company

Paignton Queens Park to Kingswear (for Dartmouth)

Next to **Paignton** station is the Paignton Queens Park station for the [Dartmouth Steam Railway & Riverboats Company](#). On departing **Paignton Queens Park** station, the steam train parallels the National Rail line for about three-quarters of a mile past Goodrington carriage sidings on the right. Soon, we reach **Goodrington Sands** station.

After leaving this station, we then pass on the left the large flumes of the [Splashdown QuayWest Water Park](#) and then inland to the right; beyond the car park is Torbay Leisure Centre and, through the trees [Paignton Zoo](#). As the train climbs, we pass the glorious sands of Goodrington beach on the left and on the right can be seen red sandstone cliffs. Soon, the beach gives way to rocky cliffs and small coves. Saltern Cove then comes into sight on the left with its contorted "Armchair" rock feature at its southern end. On the right, the red sandstone cliffs can be seen surmounted by a grass mound known as Suger Loaf Hill, which suddenly sweeps down into a small valley where Waterside Holiday Park can be seen.

There are glorious views across Tor Bay to the left, and looking out across the Bay, you can see the resort of Torquay to the left and Brixham and Berry Head to the right. On really clear days, you can even see the Isle of Portland near Weymouth rising from the sea on the horizon across Lyme Bay. The headland on the Torquay side is called Hope's Nose, and it has two rocky islands offshore, Thatcher Rock and Ore Stone. As our journey continues, the train crosses Broadsands viaduct with a panoramic view on the left of Broadsands beach. Beyond is the low headland of Churston Point, and after passing through a deep cutting, the line suddenly emerges onto the even longer Hookhills viaduct high above the bungalow estate in the valley below, leading down to Broadsands beach. Soon, the line is in a cutting again and turns away inland to reach the summit of the climb at **Churston** station which is reached after passing under the modern road bridge carrying the Paignton to Brixham and Dartmouth road.

Just before the station is the turntable on the left, and on the right is the steam railway's locomotive shed, where its fleet of steam locomotives is maintained. Also, on the left can be seen the former bay platform that was used by the branch line trains to Brixham. Today, Brixham is home to a replica of Sir Francis Drake's _Golden Hind_. _Brixham Harbour_ is also one of the major fishing ports of the South West. Brixham Harbour is also home to the historic Brixham sailing trawlers _Vigilance of Brixham_ and _Pilgrim of Brixham,_ which offer sailing trips along the South Coast.

On leaving Churston station the line then heads downhill all the way to Kingswear. The line crosses the high ground separating Tor Bay from the Dart Valley and begins dropping, at first, into deeply rolling countryside, much of it wooded, sometimes in cuttings and sometimes on embankments. Shortly after leaving Churston, we are on a high embankment with a wide view to the right over Galmpton with Dartmoor in the distance. Then follows a cutting, after which the train emerges into a small valley called Hook Bottom, curving round to Brim Hill to the right. We then cross a small stream on an embankment with a first glimpse of the River Dart at Galmpton Creek to the right through the trees. Then, we reach **Greenway Halt,** which serves Agatha Christie's Greenway House. As the train coasts gently downhill, it suddenly enters the Greenway tunnel before emerging with a really spectacular change of scenery high above the wooded slopes bordering the Dart Estuary with views right across the river upstream to Dittersham and downstream towards Dartmouth. This is *Dame Agatha Christie* country as the famous crime author lived in *Greenway House* high above the line to the right from the 1930s right until her death in 1976.

Another notable house, *Coleton Fishacre*, about a mile away, also has connections with the arts, for from 1925, it was the home of the D'Oyly Carte family, who created the *D'Oyly Carte Opera Company*. The line then crosses the Greenway viaduct and gradually drops down to river level but veers away from the shore past Longwood Creek and Noss Greek on an embankment. Noss Creek is the location of the former Philip & Sons Dartmouth shipyard but now this is the *Noss Marina*. As the train runs alongside the water's edge, a gradually expanding vista of *Dartmouth Harbour* opens out to the right with its mass of yachts and other small craft with the occasional larger vessel such as sailing ships and the odd warship. This is Onedin Line country, where many of the scenes were filmed for this famous TV series that ran from 1971 to 1980. Across the water, high on the hillside can be seen the *Britannia Royal Naval College* where all officers in the Royal Navy are trained. It is open to the public for tours via *BRNC Tours & Events*.

The train then slows down, approaching Britannia Crossing, the level crossing carrying the main road from Tor Bay to the *Higher Ferry*, seen on the right, and linking Tor Bay with Dartmouth. This is a vehicular chain ferry. The ferry is owned and operated by the Dartmouth-Kingswear Floating Bridge Company. The previous ferry boat, named *No. 7*, was built in 1960 and can carry up to 18 cars. It was unusual in that although it used chains for guidance, it was actually propelled by paddle wheels. It was built locally in the shipyard of Philip & Sons., Dartmouth and was the last surviving Diesel Electric Paddle Vessel (DEPV) in the UK. It was replaced in 2009 by a newly built ferry. It is one of three ferries across the River Dart from Kingswear to Dartmouth, the others being the *Dartmouth Steam Railway & Riverboats Company* passenger ferry and the South Hams District Council-operated *Lower Ferry,* which also is a vehicular ferry.

Then, the train continues alongside the water's edge before easing around the right-hand curve across Waterhead viaduct, with Waterhead Creek on the left and [Darthaven Marina](#) on the right, into **Kingswear** station and the journey's end. Kingswear station opened on the 16th of August 1864, and in the heyday of the Great Western Railway until the closure of the line in 1972, was the destination of the famous Torbay Express service from London Paddington. Today, the Torbay Express still runs but now terminates at Paignton. The Paignton to Kingswear line was saved in 1972 and reopened as the [Dartmouth Steam Railway & Riverboats Company](#) and is a major tourist attraction for the area. The overall roof at Kingswear station is now a listed structure and is one of only two such structures left in the country of this once common Brunel design still in railway use, the other being at Frome station.

From Kingswear you can get the [Dartmouth Steam Railway & Riverboats Company](#) passenger ferry across to Dartmouth, which runs from the landing stage alongside the station. This is reached by walking along the platform and straight ahead down to the ferry pontoon at the end of the station.

This is the successor to the railway ferry from Kingswear to Dartmouth. In 1972, BR passed the operation of the passenger ferry to the local council, but in 1977, this was, in turn, passed to Riverlink. There is also the South Hams District Council-operated [Dartmouth Lower Ferry](#) which is a vehicle ferry that runs from Kingswear to Dartmouth. This consists of a floating platform that is pushed and pulled across the river by tugs. This ferry's route runs from near Kingswear station, close to that of the passenger ferry. Kingswear is home to the [Royal Dart Yacht Club](#).

At the southern end of Kingswear rail station between the station and the ferry landing stage is the former Royal Dart Hotel which was built by the railway and was designed to accommodate passengers on the Castle Line ocean going ships that called at Dartmouth from the 1860s on their way from London bound for South Africa. These ocean going ships switched their calls to Southampton in 1891. In 1900 the Castle Line merged with the Union Steamship Company to form the Union Castle Line. It became famed for its express ocean liner service from Southampton to South Africa as well as its Round Africa service from London that alternated between going via the Suez Canal or via the Cape. Union Castle services ceased in 1977 due to the changing nature of global travel with the advent of jet airliners and the Jumbo Jet. In 2017 the former hotel after many years facing an uncertain future was converted into apartments as the Royal Dart Apartments and restored to its former glory.

Dartmouth:

Dartmouth did, in fact, have its own railway station, which is now a restaurant known as the *Platform 1 Bar & Restaurant*. The original plans for the Dartmouth & Torbay Railway line took the line across a bridge and into the town. Opposition from local seamen and merchants saw the route diverted to Kingswear on the opposite side of the river, but this occurred after the station had been built at Dartmouth. The railway, therefore, terminated at Kingswear (for Dartmouth) station and passengers transferred to Dartmouth by ferry as they still do today.

The ferry pontoon on the Dartmouth side is right outside the station building (now the *Platform 1 Bar & Restaurant*). This ferry was originally operated by the Great Western Railway and later British Rail but today is operated by *Dartmouth Steam Railway & Riverboats Company*. Dartmouth is believed to be the only place in the world with a purpose built railway station which has never seen a train.

Dartmouth is a hub for ferries and cruises around the River Dart and home to the historic paddle steamer *PS Kingswear Castle* which is operated by *Dartmouth Steam Railway & Riverboats Company* on excursion trips around the Dart and supported by the *Paddle Steamer Kingswear Castle Trust*. Dartmouth Steam Railway & Riverboats Company also operate *Dartmouth to Totnes River Cruises* and the multimodal *Round Robin Tour*. *Dittisham Ferries* operates passenger ferries from Dartmouth to Dittisham. *Dartmouth Castle Ferry* operates passenger ferries from Dartmouth to Dartmouth Castle. *Greenway & Dittisham Ferries* operates passenger ferries from Dartmouth to Greenway House.

Across the river lies the historic town of Dartmouth. Dartmouth Harbour has always been of strategic importance as a deep-water port for navy vessels. It was the home of the Royal Navy in the reign of Edward III. - ships have been built here as far back as the 12th century or earlier. Dartmouth sent many ships to join the English fleet against the Spanish Armada. The Armadas' 'payship' was captured and anchored in Dartmouth harbour. The town is home to the *Britannia Royal Naval College* which has been at the forefront of the education and development of world-class Naval Officers in Dartmouth since 1863. Dartmouth has always been of strategic importance as a deep-water port for sailing vessels (regular visits by naval and pleasure cruise vessels attest to this!). The port was used as the sailing point for the Crusades of 1147 and 1190, and Warfleet Creek, which is a short walk from Dartmouth Castle is said to be named for the vast fleets which assembled there. Dartmouth was twice surprised and sacked during the Hundred Years' War, after which the mouth of the estuary was closed every night with a great chain.

The narrow mouth of the Dart is protected by two fortified castles, [Dartmouth Castle](#) and [Kingswear Castle](#). Dartmouth is also home to the [Port of Dartmouth Royal Regatta](#) which takes place at the end of August each year and culminates spectacularly with a magnificent airshow and fireworks display.

The finest hotel in Dartmouth is the [Royal Castle Hotel](#), a favourite of the families of naval families from the Royal Naval College. A newer hotel in the town is the [Dart Marina Hotel](#) near the Higher Ferry. The town is a delightful place and gets especially busy at the time of the Passing Out Parade at the [Britannia Royal Naval College](#) and during the [Port of Dartmouth Royal Regatta](#). But Dartmouth is a beautiful town set on the wooded banks of the River Dart opposite Kingswear.

FUN FACT: DID YOU KNOW THAT…..

The Britannia Royal Naval College in Dartmouth is where Queen Elizabeth II first met Prince Philip (Duke of Edinburgh) in 1939. The 18-year-old cadet Philip was introduced to a 13-year-old Princess Elizabeth while she was touring the grounds. From then, it's said, the young royal never thought of anybody else. The two began to exchange letters throughout the war years. They married on 20 November 1947 at Westminster Abbey, starting a long married life together, which lasted over 70 years. With the death of King George VI in 1952, Princess Elizabeth became Queen Elizabeth II and reigned with her husband by her side. Together they were the stable guiding force who led Britain through changing and turbulent times, and they became global icons who were admired and respected around the world. Prince Philip passed away at Windsor Castle on 9 April 2021, aged 99, and Queen Elizabeth II passed away at Balmoral on 8 Sep 2022, aged 96. She had become Britain's longest reigning monarch, and their marriage had lasted over 70 years built on love, respect and admiration.

FUN FACT: DID YOU KNOW THAT…..

Henry Hudson was put into Dartmouth on his return from America and was promptly arrested for sailing under a foreign flag. The Pilgrim Fathers put into Dartmouth's Bayard's Cove en route from Southampton to America. They rested a while before setting off on their journey in the Mayflower and the Speedwell on the 20th of August 1620. About 300 miles west of Land's End, they realised that the Speedwell was unseaworthy and returned to Plymouth. The Mayflower departed alone to complete the crossing to Cape Cod. Dartmouth Museum tells some of this local history.

FUN FACT: DID YOU KNOW THAT…..

Thomas Newcomen, the inventor of the steam pumping engine, was born in Dartmouth in 1663. The location of his house in Lower Street is marked with a plaque, although the building itself was demolished (and reconstructed on Ridge Hill) in the nineteenth century to make way for a new road which was named after Newcomen. An eighteenth-century working Newcomen engine is on display in the town in the Newcomen Engine House.

FUN FACT: DID YOU KNOW THAT…..

In the latter part of the Second World War, the town was a base for American forces and one of the major departure points for Utah Beach in the D-Day landings. Much of the surrounding countryside was closed to the public while it was used by US troops for practise landings and manoeuvres.

FUN FACT: DID YOU KNOW THAT…..

Hindostan is the name traditionally given to the static training ship permanently moored at the Britannia Royal Naval College in Dartmouth. Hindostan is the name of the Indian Sub-Continent and the modern state of India. The current Hindostan was previously HMS Cromer, a Sandown-class minehunter that became the static training ship in 2002. HMS Cromer (M103) was built by Vosper Thornycroft in 1992. She is one of the Royal Navy's 12 Sandown class minehunters Although the class had a primary mine countermeasures role, they have had a secondary role as offshore patrol vessels. She was launched on 6 Oct 1990 and was commisioned into service with the Royal Navy on 7 April 1992. She was decommissioned from Royal Navy active service in 2001 and refitted to become a static training ship attached to the Britannia Royal Naval College in Dartmouth. For this purpose she has been renamed as Hindostan. In June 2023 she was temporarily relocated to Portsmouth while the jetties at Dartmouth were refurbished.

The Destinations

The destinations and coastal resorts served by the route include:

Torquay

Torquay is a traditional seaside resort famed for its iconic palm trees, busy harbour, international marina, sandy beach and wonderful array of continental-style cafes, restaurants and cocktail bars. Torquay is known for beaches such as Babbacombe and cliffside Oddicombe. Torquay Harbour, near the town centre, offers shops, cafes and a marina. Torre Abbey, a monastery founded in 1196, has art galleries and extensive gardens featuring plants from local writer Agatha Christie's novels.

The Western Lady Ferry has been operating a fine ferry service between Brixham & Torquay for over 75 years. The 30-minute ferry ride across the Bay to Brixham and returning to Torquay is a stress-free, delightful way to view Torbay from the sea, especially when the sun is shining!

Notable hotels in Torquay are the [Grand Hotel Torquay](#) and the [Imperial Hotel](#).

https://www.englishriviera.co.uk/explore/the-english-riviera/torquay

https://www.westernladyferry.com/

FUN FACT: DID YOU KNOW THAT…..

The Monty Python team including Cleese, visited Torquay in May 1970 to film sketches for their hugely popular TV cult series, Monty Python's Flying Circus. It was whilst staying at the Gleneagles Hotel in Asheldon Road (sadly now demolished) that the team first encountered the hotel proprietor and retired naval officer, Donald Sinclair and his wife, Beatrice. During their stay the Monty Python team experienced first-hand the eccentricities of Mr Sinclair. Most notably he berated Terry Gilliam for using his knife and fork incorrectly and threw Eric Idle's bag over a wall believing it contained a bomb (which actually turned out to be a ticking alarm clock). As a result of Sinclair's unconventional behaviour many of the Monty Python team bolted to the nearby comfortable surroundings of the Imperial Hotel. However, John Cleese decided to stay on and take notes and he invited his then wife, Connie Booth, who would become the co-writer of the series, to join him. This was to become the beginning of one of the most famous moments in British comedy history, with Donald and Beatrice Sinclair providing the inspiration for the iconic TV husband and wife characters. Only 12 episodes of Fawlty Towers were ever created, with the first series (six episodes) broadcast on BBC2 in 1975 and the second (six episodes) in 1979. It remains one of the greatest British comedy sitcoms of all time.

FUN FACT: DID YOU KNOW THAT…..

The famous British explorer Lieutenant-Colonel Percy Harrison Fawcett was born in Torquay and was believed to be the inspiration for the Indiana Jones film character. Many of his belongings are on display in the Explorers Gallery at Torquay Museum.

FUN FACT: DID YOU KNOW THAT…..

Agatha Christie was born in Torquay and remained on the English Riviera for much of her life, writing her first novel whilst working at the Dispensary in the temporary war hospital at Torquay Town Hall. She maintained close links with the English Riviera throughout her life, and as a result of her love and extensive knowledge of the area, many of her books were either set locally or inspired by the surrounding Devon scenery. Agatha's books have sold more than two billion copies and she remains the most successful female playwright of all time. The experiences, places, and people that she encountered on the English Riviera provided the inspiration for many of the characters and plots she created.

FUN FACT: DID YOU KNOW THAT…..

There are two concrete slipways at Beacon Quay in Torquay Harbour which were constructed for the embarkation of American troops for Operation Overlord from Torbay. A public piece of art was created by Bob Budd to remember the brave men who departed from here in Torquay. Stand on the cross of light in front of the D-Day Memorial and look towards the steel ring which marks the direction the troops left in. A series of lighting units in the wooden walkway spell out a secret message in Morse Code – VANISHING POINT – to remember those who did not return. The D-Day Landings were the largest seaborne invasion in history. The operation began the liberation of France, and the rest of Western Europe, and laid the foundations of the Allied victory on the Western Front.

FUN FACT: DID YOU KNOW THAT…..

During the Second World War the headland at Corbyn Head in Torquay was used as the town's main coastal battery, with huge guns in place to defend Torquay from coastal invasion. While the guns were never fired in anger, six volunteers from the Home Guard lost their lives here in 1944 when a training exercise went disastrously wrong and a shell exploded. A pyramid-shaped memorial to the men can be found on the headland dedicated not only to these six men, but a further three other Home Guards who lost their lives in bombing raids of Torquay in 1942. It also remembers the sacrifice of 1,206 Home Guards who gave their lives throughout Great Britain during the war and as such is designated a 'national' memorial to the Home Guard.

Paignton

Paignton is renowned for its long stretch of beautiful and easily accessible beachfront, promenade, traditional pier, colourful beach huts and green. Situated at the centre of Paignton seafront is Paignton Pier which is a great "All Weather" family attraction with amusements, cafe, ice creams, shops and much more. There are fine beaches including Paignton Sands itself and Broadstairs Beach between Paignton and Brixham. Paignton Harbour nestles on the western shores of Tor Bay, situated midway between Torquay and Brixham harbours.

Notable hotel in Paignton is the *Palace Hotel*.

https://www.englishriviera.co.uk/explore/the-english-riviera/paignton

FUN FACT: DID YOU KNOW THAT…..

At the outbreak of the First Word War, Oldway House, which was built on the fortunes of the Singer Corporation was offered over to the American Women's War Committee by Paris Singer who paid £5000 to convert his family home into the most opulent of military hospitals. This became the American Women's War Hospital at Oldway in Paignton. Wards of beds were housed in its grand ballroom and domed riding school, while the sweeping staircase was the entrance to an operating theatre and its ambulances were made by Rolls Royce. Over the next four years, some 7000 men were treated at Oldway, with wards named after Nancy Astor (the first female MP), Lady Paget and Lady Churchill who raised thousands to keep the hospital going.

Brixham

Brixham is accessible by bus connections (No 12 bus service operated by Stagecoach) from Paignton station. Life in the busy Devon fishing town of Brixham has always centred around the harbour, where heritage trawlers jostle for space with dayboats heading out to sea for the day's catch, bringing it home daily to Brixham's famous Fish Market, which is the largest in England. Here, in the heart of England's Seafood Coast, the freshest fish and most delicious seafood is on the menu everywhere. The Western Lady Ferry has been operating a fine ferry service between Brixham & Torquay for over 75 years. The 30-minute ferry ride across the Bay to Brixham and returning to Torquay is a stress-free, delightful way to view Torbay from the sea, especially when the sun is shining!

Notable hotel in Brixham is the *Berry Head Hotel*.

https://www.englishriviera.co.uk/explore/the-english-riviera/brixham

https://www.westernladyferry.com/

FUN FACT: DID YOU KNOW THAT…..

Brixham Trawlers' were a new design of wooden sailing trawler built in the late 18th century in Brixham. The design was adopted for use around the world and by the end of the 19th century, there were more than 3000 sailing trawlers based at British ports, with a fleet of 400 at Brixham. In the late 18th century, motivated by dwindling catches, Brixham fishermen and boat builders set about creating faster boats that could fish in deep water. The design they developed was then known as a 'Brixham Trawler' and was adopted for use around the world. It was a wooden sailing trawler, about 18-24 metres in length, with a long, straight keel. Its sleek underwater profile and tall rig gave it the speed fishermen needed to reach remote fishing grounds, towing a large trawl, and return home in relatively short time. The design of the Brixham Trawlers was copied around the British coast as new ports sprang up to take advantage of the deep-sea grounds that were opening up to faster boats. By the end of the 19th century there were more than 3000 sailing trawlers based at British ports, with a fleet of 400 at Brixham.

FUN FACT: DID YOU KNOW THAT…..

The characteristic colour of the 'red sails' used on Brixham Trawlers was the result of a preservation treatment known as 'barking'. Locally mined red ochre was combined with oil and used to coat sails to protect them from the harsh effects of seawater. It was boiled in great cauldrons together with tar, tallow and oak bark – the latter providing the name for the process. The hot mixture was painted on the sails in the barking yards at Overgang, and then hung up to dry.

FUN FACT: DID YOU KNOW THAT…..

The world's first rust prevention paint was invented in Brixham in around 1841. It was discovered by accident, as the red ochre used to dye sailing trawlers sails, inadvertently prevented rust on the ship.

FUN FACT: DID YOU KNOW THAT…..

Brixham was the landing place of William of Orange during the Glorious Revolution, and many of the town's inhabitants, who are descendants of the Dutch army, have Dutch surnames. Many of the street names in Brixham reflect the town's history, with some also bearing Dutch influences.

FUN FACT: DID YOU KNOW THAT…..

Battery Gardens in Brixham was originally built in the 16th Century to protect Brixham from the Spanish Amada, but in June 1940 this outlook became one of more than 100 armed defence batteries to be built around the UK. During the war, various guns and anti-aircraft weapons were manned by the Home Guard, which consisted of around 100 men (all over 50) doing day and night duties and living in the surrounding holiday camps. There were some 25 raids on Brixham between 1942 and 1944 and five aircraft were shot down in the Torbay area.

FUN FACT: DID YOU KNOW THAT…..

Brixham was small fishing port with a population of around 8000 people when World War Two broke out. Around 1,400 evacuees came to Brixham from London, while the town also housed a large refugee population during the war, mainly from Belgium. The Americans also arrived in numbers from 1943 onwards, with Brixham and the surrounding area used in preparation for the US forces invasion of France. The American 4th Infantry Division departed from Breakwater Beach and onto the first beach to be liberated on 6th June, code named Utah in the D-Day Landings. The D-Day Landings were the largest seaborne invasion in history. The operation began the liberation of France, and the rest of Western Europe, and laid the foundations of the Allied victory on the Western Front.

Dartmouth

Famed for both its maritime and engineering importance, Dartmouth is a town full of culture, history and heritage, from castles to forts, ancient buildings and museums. Dartmouth dates back as far as 1147, and over the centuries has managed to retain many of its original features – though now somewhat modified to fit in with modern life. Just wandering through the streets of Dartmouth, you will see an eclectic mix of architecture amongst the buildings and streets, many dating back to the 16th century, such as the Butterwalk buildings. Castles, forts and even links to the Mayflower and the founding fathers of America, Dartmouth's maritime heritage is impressive. Even today, Dartmouth is of maritime strategic importance, and is home to the Britannia Royal Naval College that trains the officers of the Royal Navy.

Notable hotels in Dartmouth are the *Royal Castle Hotel* and the *Dart Marina Hotel*.

https://discoverdartmouth.com/

https://www.dartmouthrailriver.co.uk/

https://www.greenwayferry.co.uk/

https://www.nationaltrust.org.uk/visit/devon/greenway

FUN FACT: DID YOU KNOW THAT…..

Greenway Estate is a story in its own right and is most commonly known as being the holiday home of the late great crime-novelist Agatha Christie. However, did you know that before the estate was owned by Agatha Christie, it was in fact the home of Sir Humphrey Gilbert, a pioneer of the English Colonial Empire in North America, and his half-brother Sir Walter Raleigh most famously known for bringing potatoes and tobacco to Britain.

FUN FACT: DID YOU KNOW THAT…..

Full scale rehearsals for the D-Day Landings took place at Slapton Sands near Dartmouth, due to its resemblance to Utah beach. Operation Tiger, was one of a series of large-scale rehearsals for the D-Day invasion of Normandy, which took place in April 1944 on Slapton Sands in Devon. Sadly coordination and communication problems resulted in friendly fire injuries during the exercise, and an Allied convoy positioning itself for the landing was attacked by E-boats of Nazi Germany's Kriegsmarine, resulting in the deaths of at least 749 American servicemen. Because of the impending invasion of Normandy, the incident was under the strictest secrecy at the time and was only minimally reported afterwards.

FUN FACT: DID YOU KNOW THAT…..

Dartmouth's natural advantages as a deep-water harbour of refuge, and its naval facilities and tradition, (including being the home of HMS Britannia, the Royal Navy's officer training school), made it a natural command centre and a secure base for naval actions during the Second World War. Despite being so far west, local ships played their part in the Dunkirk evacuation (Operation Dynamo), including passenger ferries that worked on the Dart and in Torbay. The evacuation of allied forces and commercial shipping from western France that followed on (Operation Aerial) is not so well known, but between June 15th and 25th in 1940 around 191,000 service personnel (British, French, Polish, Czech and Belgian forces), along with many civilian refugees, were taken by ship to the UK. Western Approaches Command based in Plymouth led the operation, and Dartmouth played its part, accommodating both ships and men fleeing France. Many were from the French Army and Navy, including 6 mine-sweepers from Brest, later taken over by the Royal Navy. Some of their crews joined the Free French Navy, while others returned to France. As Belgium fell, Dartmouth welcomed some of the Belgian fishing fleet, whose ships crammed into the harbour. Some fishing boats returned to support evacuations in Dunkirk and Biscay, while others were requisitioned and operated by the Polish Navy under Royal Navy operational command.

DEVON'S WALKING TRAILS

Devon's Walking Trails

As well as its wonderful cities, towns and coastal resorts, Devon is crisscrossed by many interesting walking trails. Here we showcase some of the notable walking trails that can be enjoyed across this beautiful county.

The South West Coast Path National Trail:

The longest of England's National Trails, the multi award-winning South West Coast Path offers 630 miles of stunning coastal walking around the entire South West peninsula. Starting at Minehead in Somerset it runs along the coastline of Exmoor, continuing along the coast of North Devon into Cornwall. It follows the entire coastline of Cornwall from Bude to Land's End and across the mouth of the River Tamar to Plymouth. From Plymouth it then continues along the south coast of Devon and it then follows the Dorset coastline before finally ending at Poole Harbour.

Https://www.nationaltrail.co.uk/en_GB/trails/south-west-coast-path/

https://www.southwestcoastpath.org.uk/

The Tamara Coast to Coast Way:

In 2023 a new 87 mile walking route that connects the south and north coasts of the South West was opened. The Tamara Coast to Coast Way follows much of the River Tamar and the boundary between Devon and Cornwall. Tamar Valley National Landscape created the route to encourage more people to enjoy this overlooked area. The route traces the course of the River Tamar from the vibrant city of Plymouth to the very source of the Tamar River near Bude.

https://www.tamarvalley-nl.org.uk/discover-explore/walking/tamara-coast-to-coast-way/

The Granite Way:

The Granite Way is an 11 mile multi-use trail running between Okehampton and Lydford along the north western edge of Dartmoor. It is mostly traffic free, largely following the route of the former Southern Region railway line. A journey along the Granite Way offers fantastic views of the granite landscape of Dartmoor, as well as a number of specific sites of geological interest. It also forms part of the National Cycle Network (NCN) Route 27 'Devon Coast to Coast' between Ilfracombe and Plymouth.

https://visitdartmoor.co.uk/get-active/cycling-on-dartmoor/the-granite-way/

The Drake's Trail:

Drake's Trail in West Devon is a 21 mile cycling and walking route linking Tavistock with Plymouth. This important part of Devon's recreational route network runs through superb countryside with attractive scenery along the western edge of Dartmoor together with much historical and heritage interest.

http://www.drakestrail.co.uk

The Tarka Trail:

Inspired by Tarka The Otter, The Tarka Trail is an 180 mile, figure eight loop exploring all the diversity and beauty North Devon has to offer. Footpaths and bridleways will take you through unspoiled countryside traversing valleys and woods through Exmoor and Dartmoor national parks. The Tarka Trail is the UK's longest, traffic-free cycle path and links Braunton in the north with Meeth in the south of the region.

https://tarkatrail.org.uk

The West Devon Way:

The West Devon Way runs for 58 km (36 mi) and the route runs from the western fringes of Dartmoor National Park moorland country then through Okehampton and Tavistock, Devon south towards Plymouth through gentler Devon countryside. It links with the Tarka Trail into North Devon. It also links with the Dartmoor Way and the Two Castles Trail.

https://visitdartmoor.co.uk/get-active/the-best-dartmoor-walks/west-devon-way/

The Dartmoor Way:

The Dartmoor Way is a long-distance footpath and cycle route centred on the Dartmoor National Park in southern Devon, England. The loop route of approximately 84 miles (135 km) that encompasses upland and moorland walking, deep Devon lanes, and also passes through towns and villages such as Okehampton, Chagford, Moretonhampstead, Buckfastleigh, Princetown and Tavistock. The Dartmoor Way links with the Tarka Trail, West Devon Way and Two Castles Trail.

https://www.dartmoorway.co.uk

The Two Castles Trail:

The Two Castles Trail is a waymarked long distance footpath in Devon and Cornwall, England. It runs for 24 miles (39 km) from Okehampton in Devon to Launceston in Cornwall, linking the two Norman castles of Okehampton and Launceston. The trail passes through the villages of Bridestowe, Lewdown and Lifton. Between Okehampton and Bridestowe, the trail coincides with the West Devon Way.

https://visitdartmoor.co.uk/get-active/the-best-dartmoor-walks/two-castles-trail/

The Two Moors Way:

The Two Moors Way was the brainchild of Joe Turner of the Two Moors Way Association and was officially opened on 29 May 1976. The original Two Moors Way route spans 102 miles from Ivybridge on the southern boundary of Dartmoor National Park to Lynmouth on the North Devon Coast in Exmoor National Park. In 2005 the Two Moors Way was linked with the Erme–Plym Trail joining Wembury on the south Devon coast to Ivybridge to create a cross-county coast-to-coast route of just over 116 miles.

https://twomoorsway.org

The East Devon Way:

The East Devon Way is a long-distance footpath in England. It runs for 38 miles (61 km) between Exmouth in East Devon and Lyme Regis in Dorset. Landscapes seen on the path include estuary, high open commons, woodlands and river valleys. The route includes some fairly steep climbs but is generally not challenging.

https://www.eastdevonway.org.uk

The Abbot's Way:

The Abbot's Way is a long distance footpath linking Tavistock with Buckfast Abbey. It is a long-distance day walk between Buckfast and Tavistock Abbeys through the southern part of Dartmoor. In medieval times there were several abbeys and monasteries around the borders of Dartmoor, but the wealthiest and most important of them were Buckfast Abbey, Plymstock Abbey and Tavistock Abbey. The monks of these abbeys were on friendly terms and often exchanged visits, making long journeys on foot across Dartmoor to do so. These journeys by the monks are the origins of the Abbot's Way.

https://visitdartmoor.co.uk/abbots-way-walk-a-long-distance-day-walk-between-buckfast-and-tavistock-abbeys/

https://www.dartmoor.gov.uk/learning/dartmoor-legends/the-legend-of-the-abbots-way

Tamar Valley Discovery Trail:

The Tamar Valley Discovery Trail connects the outskirts of Plymouth with Launceston, the ancient capital city of Cornwall. It takes in some of the most beautiful and unspoilt countryside along the way. Countryside that although tranquil now, was once a hive of industrial activity, agricultural activity, and even bloody conflict! Following the route is easy. Look for the waymarks to guide you along quiet lanes, through sleepy villages, pretty woodlands, steep valleys and lush pastureland. Along the way, you'll pass historic quays, crumbling mine-workings, and the remains of old lime kilns. Relics of the area's unique industrial heritage. For nature lovers, the tidal waters of the river estuaries are designated a Special Area of Conservation and a Site of Special Scientific Interest. You're bound to spot herons, gulls, egrets, cormorants, Canada geese and more. In recent years red kites have been spotted soaring high over the meadows too. The 31 mile long Tamar Valley Discovery Trail links Plymouth in the South with Launceston, the ancient capital of Cornwall in the North. It shares part of the Tamara Coast to Coast Way, and connects with the Two Castles Trail at Launceston.

https://www.tamarvalley-nl.org.uk/discover-explore/walking/discovery-trail/

References:

"Through the Window: The Great Western Railway from London Paddington to Penzance", GWR, 1924

"Through the Window: London Paddington to Birkenhead", GWR, 1925

"Through the Window: London Paddington to Killarney via Fishguard and Rosslare", GWR, 1926

"A Visitor's Guide to the Dart Valley Railway", 1985

"South East England by Train", Paul Atterbury, 1991

"The Golden Age of the Great Western Railway 1895-1914", Tim Bryan, 1991

"The Great Days of the GWR", David St John Thomas and Patrick Whitehouse, 1991

"Readers Digest Touring Guide to Britain", The Readers Digest, 1992

"A Visitor's Guide to the Paignton & Dartmouth Steam Railway", 1992

"Paignton & Dartmouth Steam Railway and River Dart Cruises - A Visitor's Guide", 2001

"The Great Western Railway 150 Glorious Years", Patrick Whitehouse and David St John Thomas, 2002

"Great Scenic Railways of Devon and Cornwall", Michael Pearson, 2004

"Britain from the Rails", Benedict le Vay, 2009

"Mile by Mile on Britain's Railways", S.N. Pike, 2011

"The Encyclopaedia of Titled Trains", Nick Pigott, 2012

"The Intercity Story 1964-2012", Chris Green and Mike Vincent, 2013

"Dartmouth Steam Railway - Souvenir Guide Book", 2013

"P.S. Kingswear Castle - Souvenir Guide Book", 2013

"Dartmouth River Boats - Souvenir Guide Book", 2013

"Paddle Steamer Kingswear Castle and the Steamers of the River Dart", Richard Clammer & Alan Kittridge, 2013

"Discover South Devon - Travellers Guide 2024", 2024

Image Information:

Front Cover Photo:

GWR Manor No 7827 Lydham Manor steams out of Goodrington high above the colourful beach huts on its way to Kingswear on the Dartmouth Steam Railway. (c) Alamy

p3

Photo: GWR "Speed to the West" vintage travel poster 1939. Artwork by Charles Mayo.

(c) National Railway Museum / Science Museum Group

p4

Photo: GWR Castle No 5043 Earl of Mount Edgcumbe passes Churston station on the Torbay Express on 13 September 1961. Notably this Castle class locomotive is now preserved with Vintage Trains based at Tyseley and regularly performs on the mainline.
https://vintagetrains.co.uk

(c) Colour Rail Archive

p5 Photo Montage:

Top Left: GWR Castle No 5017 The Gloucestershire Regiment 28th 61st speeds along the famed Dawlish Sea Wall with the Torbay Express on 16 June 1958. (c) Colour Rail Archive

Top Right: GWR Castle departs Churston station on the Torbay Express on 1 July 1959.

(c) Colour Rail Archive

Bottom Left: GWR Castle No 5034 Corfe Castle crosses a viaduct near Churston on the Torbay Express on 18 July 1958.

(c) Colour Rail Archive

Bottom Right: GWR Castle No 7000 Viscount Portal speeds past Teignmouth on the Torbay Express on 14 August 1957.

(c) Colour Rail Archive

p6

Photo: GWR Manor No 7827 Lydham Manor passes Goodrington Sands on a glorious summer day on the Dartmouth Steam Railway on 6 Sep 2015.

(c) Alamy

p15

Photo: Overall view of London Paddington looking towards "The Lawn" concourse.

(c) Author's Collection (6 May 2019)

p16 Photo Montage:

Top Left: Modern GWR with three Hitachi IEP trains lined up at the buffer stops at London Paddington.

(c) Author's Collection (6 May 2019)

Top Right: Statue of Isambard Kingdom Brunel on Platforms 8/9 at London Paddington.

(c) Author's Collection (6 May 2019)

Bottom Left: Statue of Paddington Bear on Platform 1 at London Paddington.

(c) Author's Collection (6 May 2019)

Bottom Right: General view along Platform 1 at London Paddington as a Hitachi IEP train awaits departure.

(c) Author's Collection (6 May 2019)

p18

Photo: General view of the Elizabeth Line platforms under London Paddington.

(c) Network Rail

p22

Photo: General view of the new station entrance at Reading following its recent rebuilding work.

(c) Network Rail

p27

Photo: View of the Westbury White Horse from the carriage window of an Intercity 125 HST.

(c) Author's Collection (6 Aug 2018)

p33:

Photo: The Castle Hotel in Taunton.

(c) Author's Collection (5 April 2015)

p34

Photo: The Museum of Somerset in Taunton.

(c) Author's Collection (5 April 2015)

p37

Photo: GWR No 3440 City of Truro rests by the Coaling Stage at Didcot Railway Centre.

(c) Author's Collection (6 May 2007)

p40

Photo: View of the Exeter Ship Canal as people enjoy the evening sunlight.

(c) Author's Collection (27 Aug 2006)

p41

Photo: Exeter Cathedral.

(c) Author's Collection (27 Aug 2006)

p42

Photo: View from the carriage window of Exeter Cathedral over the roofs of houses.

(c) Author's Collection (1 Aug 2020)

p45

Photo: Famed "GWR - 100 Years of Progress" vintage travel poster 1935 showing GWR King class No 6009 King Charles II on an express train at Dawlish near Parson's Tunnel. Artwork by Murray Secretan.

(c) National Railway Museum / Science Museum Group

p46 Photo Montage:

Top Left: View from the carriage window at Dawlish on the famous Brunel Sea Wall section.

(c) Author's Collection (27 July 2019)

Top Right: View along the railway line at Dawlish on the famous Sea Wall section.

(c) Author's Collection (21 Aug 2007)

Bottom Left: View west from the platform at Dawlish station.

(c) Author's Collection (21 Aug 2007)

Bottom Right: Dawlish station

(c) Author's Collection (21 Aug 2007)

p47

Photo: A GWR Hitachi IEP Train rounds the curve at Teignmouth to join the famous Sea Wall section.

(c) Great Western Railway (GWR)

p49 Photo Montage:

Top Left: General view of Newton Abbot rail station.

(c) Author's Collection (29 Aug 2009)

Top Right: Main entrance building at Newton Abbot rail station.

(c) Author's Collection (29 Aug 2009)

Bottom Left: Platform view at Newton Abbot station looking towards London.

(c) Author's Collection (29 Aug 2009)

Bottom Right: BR Intercity 125 HST arrives at Newton Abbot with a train bound for London.

(c) Author's Collection (29 Aug 2009)

p50

Left Photo: Torquay rail station

(c) Author's Collection (25 Aug 2009)

Right Photo: Grand Hotel Torquay (formerly known as the Great Western Hotel Torquay)

(c) Author's Collection (25 Aug 2009)

p52

Photo: Torquay GWR travel poster 1947

(c) National Railway Museum / Science Museum Group

p53

Photo: Torquay BR travel poster 1950s

(c) National Railway Museum./ Science Museum Group

p54

Left Photo: BR River Dart travel poster 1961

(c) National Railway Museum / Science Museum Group

Right Photo: GWR Sunny South Devon travel poster

(c) National Railway Museum / Science Museum Group

p55

Photo: Paignton GWR travel poster 1938

(c) National Railway Museum / Science Museum Group

P56 Photo Montage

Top Left: Paignton rail station looking towards Kingswear with the Dartmouth Steam Railway station on the left.

(c) Author's Collection (30 June 2019)

Top Right: Paignton rail station looking towards London.

(c) Author's Collection (30 June 2019)

Bottom Left: Another view of Paignton rail station looking towards London.

(c) Author's Collection (30 June 2019)

Bottom Right: General view of Paignton rail station from the level crossing.

(c) Author's Collection (30 June 2019)

P57 Photo Montage

Top Left: The Devon Belle Observation Saloon sits at the Dartmouth Steam Railway's Paignton Queens Park rail station.

(c) Author's Collection (29 June 2019)

Top Right: BR Standard No 75014 runs round the train at Paignton Queens Park rail station on the Dartmouth Steam Railway.

(c) Author's Collection (29 June 2019)

Bottom Left: General view of Paignton Queens Park rail station on the Dartmouth Steam Railway.

(c) Author's Collection (30 June 2019)

Bottom Right: View of the entrance building to Paignton Queens Park rail station on the Dartmouth Steam Railway.

(c) Author's Collection (30 June 2019)

p58

Photo: BR Standard No 75014 passes Waterside on the Dartmouth Steam Railway on 12 March 2017.

(c) Alamy

p59

Left Photo: View of Goodrington carriage sidings from the train on the Dartmouth Steam Railway.

(c) Author's Collection (30 June 2019)

Centre Photo: View of Goodrington Sands from the train on the Dartmouth Steam Railway.

(c) Author's Collection (30 June 2019)

Right Photo: View of Goodrington Sands beach from the train on the Dartmouth Steam Railway.

(c) Author's Collection (29 June 2019)

p60

Left Photo: View of Broadsands Beach from the train on the Dartmouth Steam Railway.

(c) Author's Collection (29 June 2019)

Right Photo: View of Broadsands and Tor Bay from the train on the Dartmouth Steam Railway.

(c) Author's Collection (30 June 2019)

p61

Photo: GWR Manor No 7827 Lydham Manor heads over Maypool Viaduct on the Dartmouth Steam Railway on 8 March 2024.

(c) Alamy

p62

Left Photo: GWR Manor No 7827 Lydham Manor rests outside the locomotive shed at Churston on the Dartmouth Steam Railway.

(c) Author's Collection (30 June 2019)

Right Photo: The turntable at Churston on the Dartmouth Steam Railway.

(c) Author's Collection (30 June 2019)

P64 Photo Montage
Top Left: Greenway House, former home of Dame Agatha Christie, near Dartmouth now owned by the National Trust.
(c) Author's Collection (27 Aug 2009)
Top Right: Little lookout place with canons at bottom of the garden at Greenway House.
(c) Author's Collection (27 Aug 2009)
Bottom Left: View of the River Dart from the bottom of the garden at Greenway House.
(c) Author's Collection (27 Aug 2009)
Bottom Right: The boathouse at Greenway House.
(c) Author's Collection (27 Aug 2009)

p65

Bottom Photo: The glorious approach to Kingswear from the train alongside the River Dart on the Dartmouth Steam Railway.

(c) Author's Collection (29 June 2019)

p66

Photo: BR Standard No 75014 steams into Kingswear station as seen from the train on the Dartmouth Steam Railway.

(c) Author's Collection (29 June 2019)

p67

Top Photo: Glorious view from Kingswear across the River Dart to Dartmouth and the Britannia Royal Naval College up on its hill.

(c) Author's Collection (30 June 2019)

Bottom Left Photo: BR Standard No 75014 rests at the end of its journey under the fine roof at Kingswear station on the Dartmouth Steam Railway.

(c) Author's Collection (29 June 2019)

Bottom Centre Photo: The gangway ramp down to the landing stage at Kingswear station for the ferry across to Dartmouth.

(c) Author's Collection (29 June 2019)

Bottom Right Photo: The railway station building and ferry landing stage at Dartmouth which is now converted into a restaurant / cafe. Notably Dartmouth rail station is the only rail station in the world that has never received an actual train!

(c) Author's Collection (29 June 2019)

p69 Photo Montage

Top Left: View of the platforms at Kingwear station on the Dartmouth Steam Railway with the signal box on the left.

(c) Author's Collection (30 June 2019)

Top Right: View of the platforms at Kingswear station on the Dartmouth Steam Railway.

(c) Author's Collection (30 June 2019)

Bottom Left: View towards the buffer stops under the fine roof at Kingswear station on the Dartmouth Steam Railway.

(c) Author's Collection (30 June 2019)

Bottom Right: View of the train resting in the platform at Kingswear on the Dartmouth Steam Railway.

(c) Author's Collection (30 June 2019)

p70 Photo Montage

Top Left: BR Standard No 75014 steams out of Kingswear station on the Dartmouth Steam Railway bound for Paignton.

(c) Author's Collection (1 July 2019)

Top Right: General view of Kingswear station from the public footbridge.

(c) Author's Collection (1 July 2019)

Bottom Left: General view of Kingswear station buildings.

(c) Author's Collection (1 July 2019)

Bottom Right: General view of Kingswear station buildings and frontage.

(c) Author's Collection (1 July 2019)

p71

Photo: The paddle steamer Kingswear Castle arrives at Totnes after a cruise up the River Dart from Dartmouth. This is the UK's last remaining operational coal fired paddle steamer and regularly undertakes River Explorer Cruises from Dartmouth.
https://www.kingswearcastle.org

(c) Author's Collection (20 Aug 2014)

p75

Photo: Glorious view of the River Dart from Kingswear looking up river.

(c) Author's Collection (1 July 2019)

p76

Photo: Glorious view of the River Dart, Dartmouth and the Britannia Royal Naval College from Kingswear.

(c) Author's Collection (1 July 2019)

p81

Photo: A fine view of Torquay from the Torquay Princess Pier.

(c) Author's Collection (25 Aug 2009)

p82 Photo Montage

Top Left: Torquay town centre and harbour.

(c) Author's Collection (25 Aug 2009)

Top Right: View along Torquay Princess Pier.

(c) Author's Collection (25 Aug 2009)

Bottom Left: The fine fountain and gardens along Torquay Seafront outside the Princess Theatre.

(c) Author's Collection (25 Aug 2009)

Bottom Right: View of Tor Bay from Torquay with Holland America Line's Prinsendam cruise ship anchored out in the bay.

(c) Author's Collection (25 Aug 2009)

p83

Photo: Beautiful view across Tor Bay from Torquay across to Brixham and Berry Head with the Holland America Line's Prinsendam cruise ship.

(c) Author's Collection (25 Aug 2009)

p85

Photo: Paignton Pier

(c) Author's Collection (30 June 2019)

p89

Photo: The vintage Brixham Sailing Trawler "Vigilance" sails out of Brixham Harbour on a cruise around the South Devon coast on 13 Sep 2009. https://www.vigilanceofbrixham.co.uk The Vigilance BM76 is a piece of floating history. She's one of only seven surviving sailing trawlers built in Brixham. When she was launched in 1926, she represented the pinnacle of trawler design and proved it with her record-breaking speed and by winning Brixham's coveted George V Cup in the annual Trawler Race. She returned home to Brixham in 1997 and is now lovingly restored to her former glory. She is the only trawler maintained and crewed entirely by volunteers. She is being restored so in good condition to celebrate her centenary in 2026.

(c) Alamy

p90 Photo Montage

Top Left: General view of the outer harbour at Brixham.

(c) Author's Collection (23 Aug 2008)

Top Right: General view of the inner harbour at Brixham and the Golden Hinde replica of Sir Francis Drake's famed ship.

(c) Author's Collection (23 Aug 2008)

Bottom Left: The Golden Hinde replica of Sir Francis Drake's famed ship is a visitor attraction at Brixham.

(c) Author's Collection (23 Aug 2008)

Bottom Right: View of the outer harbour and breakwater at Brixham.

(c) Author's Collection (23 Aug 2008)

p94 Photo Montage

Top Left: View of Kingswear from Dartmouth at Bayard's Cove

(c) Author's Collection (27 Aug 2009)

Top Right: View towards the mouth of the River Dart from Dartmouth.

(c) Author's Collection (27 Aug 2009)

Bottom Left: Glorious view of the River Dart looking upstream.

(c) Author's Collection (1 July 2019)

Bottom Right: View of Kingswear from Dartmouth.

(c) Author's Collection (27 Aug 2009)

p95 Photo Montage

Top Left: Royal Navy warship HMS Tyne anchored in the River Dart.

(c) Author's Collection (28 Aug 2009)

Top Right: Dartmouth Castle

(c) Author's Collection (28 Aug 2009)

Bottom Left: Mouth of the River Dart.

(c) Author's Collection (27 Aug 2009)

Bottom Right: View of Dartmouth landing stage and Dartmouth as MV Edgcumbe Belle approaches the landing stage.

(c) Author's Collection (28 Aug 2009)

p96 Photo Montage

Top Left: The former Dartmouth rail station building now converted to the Platform 1 restaurant and cafe.

(c) Author's Collection (30 June 2019)

Top Right: Dartmouth town centre with the Royal Castle Hotel.

(c) Author's Collection (30 June 2019)

Bottom Left: Dartmouth Landing Stage with the MV Cardiff Castle boat getting ready for a cruise up the River Dart to Totnes.

(c) Author's Collection (30 June 2019)

Bottom Right: Beautiful view of Dartmouth and the River Dart from the Dartmouth waterfront.

(c) Author's Collection (30 June 2019)

p97 Photo Montage

Top Left: View of Dartmouth from Dartmouth Castle with the Castle Ferry at its landing place.

(c) Author's Collection (1 July 2019)

Top Right: The two fortifications that guard the river - Dartmouth Castle with Kingswear Castle on the opposite bank.

(c) Author's Collection (1 July 2019)

Bottom Left: View of the bay from Dartmouth Castle.

(c) Author's Collection (1 July 2019)

Bottom Right: View of the two castles from the Castle Ferry landing place.

(c) Author's Collection (1 July 2019)

p98

Photo: Glorious view from Dartmouth Castle looking upstream towards Dartmouth and Kingswear with the MV Dart Venturer boat passing on a River Explorer Cruise. (c) Author's Collection (1 July 2019)

www.ingramcontent.com/pod-product-compliance
Lightning Source LLC
Chambersburg PA
CBHW042106090526
44590CB00004B/113